Facing the Storm

Portraits of Black Lives in Rural South Africa

Tim Keegan

Zed Books Ltd.
London

Ohio University Press
Athens

Facing the Storm: Portraits of Black Lives in Rural South Africa
was first published in South Africa in 1988 by David Philip, Publisher (PTY) Ltd,
217 Werdmuller Centre, Claremont 7700.

This edition published in 1988 by:

United Kingdom
Zed Books Ltd
57 Caledonian Road
London N1 9BU

United States of America
Ohio University Press
Scott Quadrangle
University of Ohio
Athens, Ohio 45701

Library of Congress Cataloging-in-Publication Data

Keegan, Timothy J.
  Facing the storm: portraits of Black lives in rural South Africa
/ Tim Keegan.
      p.   cm.
  ISBN 0-8214-0924-7. ISBN 0-8214-0925-5 (pbk.)
    1. South Africa—Rural conditions—Case studies. 2. Blacks—South
Africa—Social conditions—Case studies. I. Title.
HN801.A8K44 1989
305.8′96088—dc19

British Library Cataloguing in Publication Data

Keegan, Tim, *1952-*
  Facing the storm : portraits of black lives
  in South Africa.
  1. South Africa. Black persons. Racial
  discrimination by society, to
  1980. Socioeconomic aspects
  I. Title
  305.8′968

  ISBN 0-86232-824-1
  ISBN 0-86232-825-X pbk

Contents

Preface

This book tells the story of four black South Africans who lived and worked in the countryside, on the highveld, during the course of this century. It is a history of mostly obscure, ill-educated people, whose lives are unknown to most of their compatriots, but deserve telling, not only for their own sake but also because their experiences have been shared by many others like them. Using oral interviews conducted with them, I have tried to reconstruct and record their lives as faithfully and vividly as I could, in the hope that their experiences as individuals, as blacks in a white-dominated South Africa, and as peasants, sharecroppers, farmers, tenants and labourers, will become more widely known and understood. This book, then, is a people's history, a history of ordinary black folk, but it is also more. It is concerned as well to investigate wider themes of social and economic change by examining the lives of a handful of individuals.

These life stories were collected as part of the Oral Documentation Project of the African Studies Institute, University of the Witwatersrand, Johannesburg. Started in 1979 by Professor Charles van Onselen, the project has employed several field workers over the years to record the life stories of elderly black folk, wherever they are to be found in the townships and rural areas of the highveld region. The project has always had a rural focus in the belief that the rural experience of black people crucially needs to be understood. The collections now amount to several hundred tapes, the best of which have been transcribed and translated into English. Those included here are a trifling few, selected for the crucial issues they raise and their value in illustrating the incomparable worth of such evidence in illuminating dark corners of the South African experience. My hope is that they will be read by many people with an intelligent interest in the black experience, and in the ways (still largely undocumented) in which present-day South Africa emerged.

PART ONE

Ndae Makume (photo: African Studies Institute)

The Life Story of Ndae Makume

Viljoensdrif is a hot place, in the middle of the South African highveld. It is the place at which the railway line from the Cape crosses the Vaal River. There are a few shabby railwaymen's houses, a dusty police station, a cluster of impermanent-looking buildings containing a black junior school, and an erratic spread of gum trees to indicate the proximity of water. Unless you are especially observant you could pass through without realising that a river of some size meanders nearby. Dirty trails of smoke skirt the horizon, excreted from the collieries and refineries of the industrial towns in the vicinity. For the rest, the landscape is flat: flat and unengaging. But it is across this hot, flat, unengaging landscape that the great drama of South Africa has been played out. Ndae Makume knows that; for that is where he lived.

We went seeking Ndae there in May 1984. Through the broken windows of the school we saw the black children chanting away, their words echoing out past the forlorn gum trees, across the endlessly flat fields of stubble – the remains of last year's maize crop, perhaps destroyed by drought before it could be garnered. But Ndae Makume's church of corrugated iron, built in 1898, had disappeared as if it had never existed. Some rubble, overgrown with long grass, was all that remained to remind us that, once, here was a building, a mission, a faith, a community, a church. The 'Board' had come, we were informed by the black head of the school, his moist, earnest face set off by his shining, worn suit. They had pulled down the church, and the old man had been carried off to Sebokeng in the back of a truck. Whatever happened to his cows, his dilapidated yokes, his rusted harrows and ploughs, we never discovered. When we eventually found him a few weeks later, sitting alone in his grandson's small house, he was a tired shadow of himself, tired and worn out: a tired old man, wondering behind his listless eyes what we wanted of him. He remembered us; he remembered Flatela who had first visited him; he was prepared to talk to us again. It seemed that the past no longer interested him: the future less so. But as we probed with our rude, ignorant, intrusive questions, something of his old enthusiasm for the past returned. When we went back, hoping to find him in better spirits, he was dead.

I remember Ndae as a big bear of a man in brown overalls, tending his motley herd of cows at Viljoensdrif. When I met him he was past 80, keen, interested, with a delight in talking of his and his forefathers' lives. He died as he had lived – an obscure, uneducated old man who could not be traced by the local Administration Board officials in Sebokeng because they had too much else to do. But the obscure story of his life encapsulates a whole world of social experience which exists only in the memories of old men and women, and which finds no echo at all in the conventional, narrow sources of evidence on which we rely for our more formalised image of the past. For that reason alone, it is worth recording.

*   *   *

Family memory has it that the original bearer of the Makume name was a Motaung, who had his eyes pierced out during the wars of the Difaqane by the Batlokoa marauders – the original 'Mantatees' of colonial mythology, led by their legendary warrior queen Mantatisi (whose reputation as a woman of massive proportions with flowing locks and giant ears belies her real achievements). This dastardly deed was supposedly avenged by the Bataung chief Moletsane. Ndae Makume's great-great-grandfather, Nkgatho, fought under Moletsane as an ally of Moshoeshoe in his wars against the burghers of the Orange Free State Republic in the 1860s, participating in the battle of Thaba Bosiu in which the Boer hero Louw Wepener was killed; and Ndae particularly remembers the stories told him of *Ntoa ea Dihela* – 'the war of self-destruction' – when Moroka's Barolong from Thaba Nchu, the traditional allies of the Boers, threw themselves down the sandstone cliffs rather than be killed by the Bataung.

After the Caledon River was established as the border of a truncated Lesotho in 1868, the Bataung, including the Makume lineage, lost their lands around Mekoatleng mission station on the Orange Free State side of the border, and found themselves inside the boundaries of Moshoeshoe's state. The Makumes, like so many others in Lesotho, moved back out of the Matsieng area of Lesotho into the Orange Free State well before the turn of the century – during the wars of Lerotholi and Masopha in Ndae's memory, meaning probably the civil strife of the early 1880s. The growth of an intensive cash-crop economy in the fertile Lesotho lowlands, particularly after the opening of the Griqualand West diamond fields, exacerbated the land shortage. The possibilities for re-establishing an independent productive base on the farms of the Orange Free State, free of chiefly exactions, but at the cost of entering tenancy agreements with white landholders, were very inviting. This large kin group migrated with their livestock, bringing with them sickles and shears in order to perform piece work on the farms as they travelled, and thus earn some money or enlarge their herds with the odd bullock.

The group consisted of Ndae's great-grandfather Motetesi and his brother Sefako and their respective families. Motetesi's sons were Mohlakala (Ndae's grandfather), Gafa and Mosimane. Sefako's sons were Taunyana, Koeranta and Tebellong. Motetesi, whom Ndae (born in 1903) remembers well, could never speak the white man's tongue, and horrified his sons by loudly proclaiming on their arrival at a white farmhouse, 'What is this Hottentot saying? It seems that these Hottentots are problematical.' They lived for some time on a farm remembered as Phofong, belonging to Chrisjan Esterhuys in the Ladybrand district, where they could graze their cattle, horses, sheep and goats, and cultivate wheat, maize and beans (but not sorghum, which they bought as the soil was not suitable for it). In return, they ploughed for Esterhuys, and tended and sheared his sheep. But the family was not yet as wealthy as it was to become.

Ndae's father, Molefe, married a distant cousin, a daughter of Teletsane, once they had arrived in the Lindley district of the Orange Free State. Ndae was born on 2 February 1903 on Karel Serfontein's farm near the later town of Edenville. He was the youngest of six sons. Significantly perhaps, he refers to his brothers by their Afrikaans rather than their Basotho names (Jan, Andries, Izak, Piet and Abel). Ndae himself was always known to whites throughout his life as Jacob. The only

6

one born after him (in 1905) was his sister Elizabeth, who married a Rampai and died a few years before Ndae.

Ndae's earliest memories are of life on the land of Christiaan Rabie, where they settled soon after Ndae was born. Rabie had an extensive transport business, carrying consignments from the railway line to the stores in the small towns of the region. He only wanted people on his land who could tend and drive his spans of oxen. But as he hired a number of grazing farms, strategically situated to enable his transport wagons to take on new spans on their journeys between towns and railway stations, those in his employ had no shortage of land for their own farming enterprises too. Rabie had fourteen ox wagons on the road, sometimes requiring five different spans of oxen each for one round trip. The wagons would load up at Kroonstad or Lindley Road stations (on the main Cape–Johannesburg, and the connecting line to Natal from Kroonstad respectively) and carry their loads to Lindley, Senekal, Reitz or Heilbron. Wagon space was hired by the small storekeepers and others to whom goods had been consigned by rail. Bags of maize and bales of wool would be carried on the return journey to the railway. Rabie also had the postal contract for the surrounding districts, and his horse-drawn carts distributed the mails to the postal agencies.

The Makumes lived at Brandhoek near the town of Lindley, a farm Rabie hired to provide grazing for his trek oxen between trips. Ndae's father and his four uncles and their cousins were employed as span drivers. His great-grandfather Motetesi was still the patriarch of the kin group and in charge of its farming activities. Living in a nearby homestead on the farm was the Teletsane family, also of the Bataung clan, but of a

7

senior lineage to the Makumes.

The family's cattle resources were not very considerable at the time, as Ndae's uncles were getting married, and bridewealth (*bohali*) commonly amounted to twenty head at the time. He thinks the family's cattle resources amounted to about thirty head on average during their years on Rabie's farm. Ndae remembers as a child helping to weed the fields, milking the family's cows, loading cream, butter and eggs on horse carts to be taken and sold in Lindley, and accompanying the carts into town. But it was while in Rabie's employ that the Makumes split up. Ndae's great-grandfather's brother Sefako and his sons and their families moved eastward to settle at Skietmekaar, a farm belonging to one Naudé. Now that Ndae's father's generation was marrying and producing families, the kin group was becoming very large and fission seemed inevitable. This was a process that was taking place commonly on the farms, and the day would come when the large homesteads would disappear completely in the arable districts of the highveld. But for the Makumes that day was still far off.

Ndae's father earned a widespread reputation as an expert in training and handling spans of oxen, and won for himself the sobriquet Jan Drywer amongst the whites of the district. Properly constructed bridges were few and roads primitive. Considerable skill was required in getting cargoes safely over the many gullies and streams. Jan Drywer was often called out to help some rider whose wagon had got stuck in the sands, and Ndae occasionally accompanied him. 'He knew how to make the oxen co-ordinate their pulling strength,' says Ndae.

'My father would ask the driver to talk to the span in his own style to pull. Then the man would try to make the span move but to no avail. Then my father would tell him to wait. He would then start changing the positions of the oxen in the span by taking perhaps one from the front and inspanning it in the middle, one from the back was moved to the front, and so on. After this he would take the whip and start calling out to the span to be ready to pull. He would move towards the back and clap the whip as if he were giving those at the back a spur, then he would go to the ones in the front and do the same thing, and he would then move to the middle of the span shouting and howling; then he would jump backwards and stand there shouting. To everyone's surprise and amazement, the span would pull that wagon out of the donga and on they would move.'

Makume never struck his oxen but always issued orders to them by their individual names.

Another vivid memory that remains with Ndae from the years of his youth was of the older men sitting around the evening fire tanning animal hides. Sharpened spikes from umbrellas would be used to break the blood vessels and prevent the hides from drying and becoming hard; then ox brains would be smeared on the hides to soften them. 'The group would kneel on the ground and while singing they would prick the hides with these sharpened spikes until they became soft, smearing them with this brain fat.' Blankets, women's dresses and coats would be made from the tanned hides.

But Ndae has less pleasant memories of farm life as well. He particularly remembers the stories told of the Wessels brothers, elected field cornets in the Lindley district, whose reputation for extreme cruelty was widely reported. White farmers commonly relied on the Wesselses' informal brand of justice to strike terror in the hearts of recalcitrant tenant workers. Blacks who had incurred the wrath of their employers would be sent to the Wessels farm with a note placed within the crack of a split piece of wood, in which the victim's misdemeanours were spelled out.

'It may have happened that you contradicted what the white man said, as if you were on the same level as he; then you would be given a letter to be taken to Baas So-and-so. He would read the letter, after which he would ask you to go into the storeroom to help his people clear up, and you would go without suspicion. Whilst busy there, they would come in, a group of strong white men, and they would ask you where you got the right to talk like that to a Baas. You would try to explain, but they would insist on asking you where you got the right. They would then hold you and make you lie with your stomach on a wine barrel – those old wooden ones. Around the barrel they would nail pegs in the ground, two in front of your head and two behind. They would then tie your hands and feet to these pegs with a piece of rope. They would take a *borsketting* – the strap that goes round the chest of a horse when it is pulling a cart. You could find yourself being beaten by one person, but with these cornets it was usual for four whites to punish you. They would hit you so severely that your bowels would work and the whole place would be a mess. After such a beating the victim had to be carried home and was unable to walk. Even sitting was difficult and your family would have to nurse you for some time before you could resume work. A victim of such treatment would sleep on his stomach for up to three weeks. Those Boers knew their job.'

Ndae remembers hearing of people who died after falling victim to the field cornets. Often there was no reason given for such punishment. 'If they were afraid of you and thought you were strong and bold they would just make you work hard, and if you grumbled or displayed some unwillingness to do what you had been ordered to do, they would punish you. . . . That is why the old people who lived on the farms in those days are so afraid of the white man; we think much of such things.'

But the inexorable grip of white domination was all the time gathering around the Makumes. The first time that they began to experience the intensifying forces arrayed against rural blacks was in 1913, a year of crisis in relationships between black and white on the land. This was the year of the 'great dispersal' in the Orange Free State arable districts, when white farmers, taking advantage of the 1913 Natives Land Act of that year, launched a concerted, collective effort to change the terms of tenancy in their favour, and greatly to extend their control over the labour, the resources and the productive enterprise of blacks living on their land. Perhaps Ndae was too young (he was 10 at the time) to recall the exact circumstances of the family's move away from Rabie's employ. It is likely that white farming in the vicinity was becoming more intensive and capitalised, and the wide-open spaces of past years were becoming fenced in. Rabie sold his business shortly hereafter, so it is also possible that the leases on his farms were expiring. But Ndae does recall vividly that their move at this time was caused in part by the forced sale of their goats. Goats were regarded as especially destructive creatures, as they tended to wander into nearby orchards and nibble at the young shoots. The Makumes were obliged to sell their fifty or so goats to travelling speculators, taking advantage of the plight of the blacks on the farms, for some 10 shillings each.

Thus in 1913 the Makumes reaped their crop,

gathered their livestock, their goods and chattels, loaded their ox wagons and left Rabie's employ. As was the case throughout the arable districts in the winter of 1913, many of the tenants in the neighbourhood were also turned off the land rather than submit to the demands and exactions of landlords. 'They started scattering in all directions,' recalls Ndae. As the Makumes trekked to their new farm, Kleinfontein, they came across many others on the road, moving from one tenancy to another; but unlike the Makumes, most of them were unlikely to find better terms than those they had left behind.

Ndae's father and uncle Sefako had already entered an agreement with their new landlord, Danie Doubell, to move on to his land. 'When a group intended moving,' says Ndae, 'they sent out at least two members to go and negotiate accommodation with landowners first. Once this had been obtained, they came back to the family group to report this and then the trek began.' Doubell was impressed by the Makumes' credentials as trainers and handlers of animals, as reflected in the testimonial written by Rabie on their 'trek pass'. He was prepared to allow the entire kin group of four generations to settle on his land. He lent them a wagon and a span of oxen to supplement their own to help transport their possessions. Two trips were required by each wagon to complete the move.

Not surprisingly, the trek to Doubell's farm features large in Ndae's early memories. He remembers the outspan on Jan Swanepoel's farm; he recalls collecting dry cow dung for fuel and water for cooking. He remembers sleeping under the wagon, its wheels chocked with stones to prevent it from moving, and the sleeping oxen lying nearby, fastened to the yoke to prevent them from trudging off into the night. On their arrival at Kleinfontein the next afternoon, the entire family had to go and 'greet the king' – Danie Doubell, to whom they were each introduced by name. Doubell, to whom Ndae habitually refers as Danie and who was known to the Basotho as 'Sebata sa Mampabale', was a patriarchal figure who loomed large in Ndae's young life. He had lived in Lesotho for a long time, buying Basotho horses for resale on the diamond fields of Griqualand West, and had learned to speak Sesotho as well as something of Basotho law. He applied justice to his Basotho tenants in much the same way as a chief might, ordering for instance that the father of a seduced girl be compensated with six head of cattle, which he chose himself from the guilty party's herds. He would say to the girl's father after listening to all evidence, 'Take these now and get your men to help you brand them with your own mark.'

Doubell's farming operations were, it is clear, highly capitalised by the standards of the day. His imported breeds of woolled sheep were shown at the local agricultural shows, and farmers came from far and near to buy lambs born of his imported ewes. These special sheep, which grazed close to Doubell's homestead, were not allowed to get wet in the rain; they had to be covered with special coats whenever rain threatened. 'Even in handling them, we were not supposed to grab them anyhow; Danie would be very cross if he saw you doing that. Their bodies were not to be touched by hand; we had to hold them by their legs.' Ndae still expresses his amazement at the fecundity of Danie's milk cows, imported from Holland, which were milked three times a day and yielded five gallons each milking. Other farmers in the district sold him their milk, as Danie had cheese-making machinery, and exported his cheese to

England to feed the troops during the First World War. Those farmers in the district who were not sympathetic towards the imperial war effort refused to sell Danie their milk, Ndae remembers. The plant was worked by men whose language was incomprehensible to Ndae, indicating to him that they were Englishmen. He also remembers helping to load cheese on a cart pulled by eight mules, which took it to Lovat station. After the war the machinery was dismantled and sent back to England.

The size of Doubell's landholdings was such that no real limit was placed on the extent of the land available to the Makume family for grazing and ploughing. By the First World War this was a most unusual situation on the highveld. Only the luckiest – or the most valuable – black families could still hope by 1913 to have access to the landed resources available to the Makumes. Doubell, who was undoubtedly a very wealthy man, owned (or hired) a number of farms – stretching in Ndae's memory from near Lindley to close to Steynsrus, a distance of perhaps twenty miles. 'This was not a farm but the whole world,' enthuses Ndae.

It was at Kleinfontein that the Makumes' stockholdings became very large, especially when they exchanged their horses for cattle. Ndae remembers that the family owned 170 head of cattle and over 500 sheep. The animals were all regarded as being under the control and authority of the family head, no matter who had earned them. Their wool was despatched to Durban from Lindley Road station, fetching about 1s 6d per pound. They also made butter and sold it at the station. The only restriction on the black-owned livestock was that they were not allowed near Danie's herds and flocks. Danie loaned his bulls to his tenants on condition the

Africans did not keep their own bulls which might get amongst his prize cows.

Furthermore, seven or eight hundred bags of maize and sorghum from the family's fields were not unheard of in good years. It took four months to plough the land – from September to December. They would plough every day except Sunday until late in the evening. Ndae remembers beer being brewed and meat cooked to pay the harvesters who flocked to their fields in the winter. Danie would loan them a threshing machine. By now the Makumes also owned two *bokwae* – transport wagons pulled by fourteen oxen each, which cost 125 pounds new, as well as two horse carts which they hired out for weddings to other tenant families. Although sharecropping relationships between black tenants and white landholders were common in the district, they were not practised on Danie's lands. Sharecropping was more likely to be found on the farms of less prosperous and undercapitalised white landholders.

The young Ndae began working in the fields as an adolescent, feeding Danie's horses, helping with the ploughing and herding the calves, in about 1914. He remembers working in a group of sixteen youths (perhaps all from the same kin group) who lived together closer to their employer's farm house, while the Makume homestead and fields were situated much further away, on the other side of the Vals River. The older members of the extended family did not render labour, but paid for their tenancy with the labour service of their juniors. Amongst those living nearby, also on Doubell's land, was the Teletsane family, also of the Bataung clan, of whom Ndae's mother was a member. It might have been the Teletsanes who lured the Makumes to Kleinfontein in the first place; and their success as arable farmers might have had more than a little to do with the larger network of kin already established there.

Ndae's father, Jan Drywer, did much of the transport work on Danie's land, in between attending to the family's extensive farming activities. He also seems to have had a particularly close relationship with their landlord. He was called upon to advise on the adjustment of the ploughs or the arrangement of the ploughing spans. He was called in to fix the ploughing equipment or to sharpen the shares. Danie would bring Ndae's father a sheep as a Christmas present, saying, *'Hier is jou skaap, ou Drywer.'* Ndae remembers others on the farm were hurt by Danie's acts of benevolence, and suspected Ndae's father of currying favour.

Such relationships of convenience between wealthy white farmers with very extensive and underutilised landholdings, and black kin groups controlling considerable labour resources, were still to be found in parts of the arable highveld into the 1920s. Nevertheless, these relationships, allowing to the black homestead community access to considerable landed resources (as well as occasional access to seed or the services of a threshing machine), and guaranteeing to the landlord access to a steady and dependable supply of labour from the junior members of tenant families, were already becoming rarer and more and more tenuous. As land was subdivided, so white-directed farming became more intensive and the resources available to black tenants declined. As pressures were brought to bear on tenants' own productive activities, as the village settlements of the extended black kin groups were broken up and the nuclear family became more common as a unit of tenancy on the farms, so the authority of elders over juniors eroded and the shift of young men and women away from unremunerative and exploitative employment on the farms to the towns became a steady flow.

Portents of things to come appeared when Danie started apportioning his farms to his children. It was not long after the First World War ended, Ndae thinks, that the land on which the Makumes lived fell under the control of Danie's son-in-law, a Hollander named Fritz Richter. They were invited to move so as to remain under Danie's control, but decided to remain where they were. At first this development did not greatly change the family's circumstances. By now Ndae's great-grandfather Motetesi had died at a great age, and his son Mohlakala, Ndae's grandfather, had become the senior patriarch of the family group, in name as well as in fact.

The division of Danie's land was accompanied by the division of the wild herd of blesbok which roamed over Danie's land. The herd was chased by a posse of mounted men, black and white, until it split in two. One part of the herd was then driven onto Richter's land, and fencing was erected to prevent the herd from reuniting. This was a common practice as the substantial landholdings of an earlier date were subdivided, according to Ndae. Richter got from his father-in-law 200 blesbok, as well as 2 000 sheep, two ox wagons and four spans of oxen. It was not long before the inexorable process of subdivision advanced a further step, when Richter's son-in-law, Willie Austen, a Scot, became the Makumes' landlord. Although Austen called his farm Kismet, to the Makumes their home remained known as Kleinfontein. The extensive tracts of yore were becoming more and more crowded.

In 1924 Ndae married Anna, the daughter of one Mokoita, a Mokoena of Molibeli descent, who lived on a nearby farm further up the Vals River, belonging to Gert

Meyer, a cousin of Danie Doubell. The bridewealth cattle were mostly provided by Mohlakala, Ndae's grandfather. In October of the following year they confirmed their marriage by Christian rites. Ndae's new wife moved permanently to his parental homestead. In May 1926 their first child – a girl – was born. When asked if this meant that he became independent of parental authority, Ndae dissents vigorously:

'No, it was still one combined family. . . . Children of olden days used not to leave their parents immediately after getting married. They were supposed to stay on and work under their parents' authority. Even your wife was supposed to stay with your parents and cook for them. We had a separate hut where I slept with my wife, but during the day she had to work at my parents' home. In those days my wife was regarded as my elders' wife, not mine. The old man had authority over both of us.'

However, the fortunes of the Makume family really began to change at about this time. Ndae recalls that it was after General Hertzog's government came to power in 1924 that blacks were forced to dispose of their animals on the farms. Africans had to sell off their cattle, except for a couple of milk cows and perhaps some draught oxen. Newly born calves had to be sold. Only one horse was allowed to blacks who did not own carts. Ndae recalls that inspectors (quite probably census enumerators) came around counting how many cattle, sheep, goats and horses the black farm tenants had.

The terms of tenancy increasingly being imposed upon blacks, as described by Ndae, precluded any independent production, but payment for labour took the form of the produce of a couple of acres, ploughed in common with the landlord's fields under the landlord's direction, the produce of which would belong to the tenant worker. The produce of a couple of acres might be fifteen or sometimes twenty bags of maize. Black tenants also received money wages – 15 or 20 shillings for a month's work, 5 shillings per month for boys, 2s 6d per month for girls employed in the kitchens. 'That was the death of the black people,' in Ndae's memory. 'What else could they do? If a person expressed dissatisfaction, where could he go? It was better to keep quiet rather than talk. There was no longer any opportunity to plough as we liked. Those big tracts of land we used to plough were a thing of the past.'

Ndae's memories in this regard are no doubt exaggeratedly apocalyptic. But in the longer term these were the changes that his people were experiencing. Needless to say, though, such experiences were not universal; many a white landholder did not possess the capital resources (and others did not have the incentive) to seek to do away entirely with the productive equipment and oxen of their black tenants – as Ndae's future life was to show. The dispossession of blacks went hand in hand with the accumulation of productive capacity in the white rural economy (a function to a large degree of government succour); and white accumulation was never sustained indefinitely, as the years of the Depression were to demonstrate.

Nevertheless, the second half of the 1920s (like the years leading up to the First World War) were years when the advance of white farming and the retreat of the black peasant economy took on dramatic dimensions. By the mid-1920s white agriculture on the highveld was entering a renewed phase of boom and expansion. The coming to power of the National Party, with its strong populist roots in the Orange Free State countryside, might have provided the moral impulse for white landholders seeking to extend control over the land and over the black families on the land; and elderly informants like Ndae commonly ascribe to Hertzog's government transitions in their experiences of life on the farms that were rather more complex in their causation. An example of this tendency is Ndae's assertion that it was as a result of Hertzog's 'cruel laws' that at this time the prices they received for their maize collapsed, to 6 or 7 shillings per bag. But this might have been due to the fact that one aspect of the tightening control blacks were experiencing was the insistence that they sell their produce to their landlords rather than to the store-keepers in the rural towns and at the railway stations. This enabled the landlords to make an extra profit from paying their tenants below market prices, and also enabled them to exert greater control over the mobility of tenants and their tenants' ability to profit from other forms of petty trade. This change was certainly taking place over the longer term, but it is quite likely that there were particular moments of heightened conflict, such as the mid-to-late 1920s, when whites were able decisively to extend their control over blacks in this way.

Another reason for the gradually narrowing opportunities for profitable farming experienced by the Makumes was the fact that the old landlord, Danie Doubell, was now dead. Not untypically, the younger generation of white farmers was less inclined to tolerate large settlements of relatively well-off black farmers on their land – not only because they used landed resources which could more profitably be put to alternative use, but also because of the moral opprobrium against 'Kaffir farming' and against whites who lived off it. This sense of moral outrage had been assiduously preached by Afrikaner leaders, particularly in Hertzog's National Party.

Ndae says that Danie's sons and sons-in-law had been indoctrinated against the blacks on their land, that they were jealous of black successes, and that they were determined to rob the black tenants of their freedom.

'Now it was the sons who wielded power, and Hertzog had influenced them by saying that if they kept on allowing us to plough and practise pastoral farming on our own, it would not be long before we took those farms away from them. . . . They were called to meetings and at those meetings they were so brainwashed that when they came back they would tell us, "From now on, you cannot keep cattle on the farm; you must plough and work for us, and whoever does not understand that had better leave this place." . . . It was about 1926 and 1927 when the world changed for us. Those were bad times.'

There was no open hostility shown toward them – 'because after all we grew up together; they simply said your possessions are too many, you would be wise to try and find another place.' Under these pressures the Makume family group began to break up, with individuals moving off with some of the livestock to seek tenancies elsewhere. By distributing their animals in various places in this way, they hoped to protect them against forced sales or death through shortage of grazing. Ndae's father and elder brothers moved back to Kleinfontein in 1933, after spending a few years in the employ of Jakob Rotten. (Mohlakala was now dead.) Austen welcomed them back to their old home, insisting that he had never told them they should leave, but only to get rid of their livestock. Ndae still regards Kleinfontein as his family home, and there many of the Makumes lie buried. 'Whenever I return there,' says Ndae, 'I take my hat off.'

This period coincided with Ndae's conversion to the

African Methodist Episcopal Church, a powerful separatist black church founded in and run from the United States. It is likely that the timing of this conversion, in 1926, was not fortuitous, for the AME Church was born out of black nationalist ideals, and it seems to have grown most rapidly as a political and cultural expression at precisely such times of disillusionment with the white man's world and the white man's values. Many blacks on the land had to some degree imbibed ideas of individual self-improvement through diligence and effort. When such avenues seemed to be closing as a consequence of white hostility and greed, new forms of political and religious expression arose to accommodate the sense of disillusionment and lost pride which resulted. The AME Church was one such expression, and not surprisingly one that was increasingly regarded with suspicion and intolerance by whites.

Another such expression which Ndae remembers vividly and which further provoked whites to take concerted action against their black tenants, was Clements Kadalie's Industrial and Commercial Workers' Union, the first mass black trade union in South Africa, which had a spectacular if short-lived success in mobilising support in rural areas. The farm tenantry was ripe for political mobilisation at this time. Ndae remembers that many of the tenants donated cattle to Kadalie's organisation, and his representatives held meetings on the farms. It was at such gatherings that Ndae like so many others had their first schooling in the large historical forces confronting them and shaping their lives. Kadalie's appeal was unashamedly messianic in Ndae's memory. The whites had taken their country and they should fight to repossess it, they were told. 'I have come to take you out of Egypt,' was the message. Perhaps inevitably, this heady experience was not to last, given the general insecurity of farm life and the hostility of the whites. The level of self-confidence required to sustain such a movement could not long survive the dispossession of resources and the undermining of their economic independence which confronted blacks on the land.

But there is no limit to the determination of the strong-willed to survive in the face of hopelessness. One of Ndae's clearer memories of this period is the year he and his father hired a government-owned farm in Lindley district by getting a white man – an impoverished blacksmith in Lindley – to hire the farm for them in his name, on which to plough and graze their livestock. The rent amounted to 360 pounds per annum. Of this they handed over 180 pounds to the white man, Lood-Jan Graaff, with which to pay the first instalment. Ndae got two ploughing spans of oxen from his relations. He remembers the farm as 'fertile and beautiful with a stream running through it'. It was the best farm in the area, asserts Ndae with perhaps a touch of retrospective exaggeration, and was capable of producing 2 000 bags of maize. But the arrangement did not last. Ndae remembers: 'I suspect that while I was ploughing, some whites became suspicious and started investigating. They employed the services of a lawyer, a certain De Wet, and we were called to court to answer their allegations about that farm and the nature of my involvement.'

It was alleged that the poor white, Graaff, could not possibly have paid the rent himself as he had no money, that Ndae had in fact paid the 180 pound instalment, and that the spans and equipment being used for ploughing belonged to Ndae too. In fact, even the two cows which supplied Graaff with his daily milk belonged to the Makumes, and they had been lent to him for this purpose. The lease was cancelled, and Ndae was turned off the farm. Ndae lost his 180 pounds. He and Graaff commiserated with each other, Ndae took the cows back, and they parted.

The ambiguities of white supremacy were forcibly brought home to Ndae by this episode; for the lawyer De Wet came up to him afterwards and 'told me that I should have consulted him first and he would have leased that farm for me, and nobody would question it because he was a lawyer and had money. It was too late because my money was gone already.'

The magistrate, too, told Ndae that he should have leased the farm 'through the lawyers', and that his mistake had been to rely on a poor white. Clearly what Ndae had done was formally illegal according to the 1913 Natives Land Act; hiring or buying land was a privilege for whites only. It was also in flagrant opposition to populist white perceptions of the proper relations between white and black on the land. But there can be no doubt that such relationships between black farmers and white landholders were not uncommon at this time, and were often connived at by the absentee landowners who knew that black tenants, ploughing typically under informal sharing contracts, were reliable and productive farmers. Law in a racially ordered society is often a symbol rather than a practical code regulating real relationships. De Wet and the magistrate knew this, and Ndae knew it too. As long as whites (lawyers were as well-placed as any) were able to make profits from black tenant enterprise by sharing in the harvest, the law was a flexible tool at best. But Ndae had erred in flouting the rules of class privilege in the white rural community by turning to a poor white as his partner and as the beneficiary of his enterprise.

These were the sorts of arrangements which remained available to enterprising black farmers in the interstices of the white-controlled rural capitalism emerging in the 1920s. By their very nature they were also very insecure and temporary arrangements in a world overwhelmingly hostile to any sign of independent economic enterprise by blacks. But the blacks were not without weapons of their own. Ndae recalls a quarrel he had with a certain Pretorius whose land he had agreed to plough with his own oxen and equipment, in return for the yield from two bags of maize seed – amounting to one third of the crop. After threshing, Ndae claimed 330 bags as his own. But Pretorius allowed him to take only 200 bags, declaring that he would give him nothing more. Pretorius hired a transport rider, Izak Botha, to carry the remainder to the co-operative overnight without Ndae's knowledge. However, Ndae was now wise in the ways of the white man's law, and had obliged Pretorius to write down the agreement and append his signature to it. He also knew a lawyer named Ellenberger, a scion of a French missionary family from Lesotho, who in Ndae's words 'did not care about Boers'. Ellenberger told Ndae that the case was clear-cut and took the matter to the local magistrate's court in Lindley (perhaps to the same official who had ordered Ndae off the government-owned farm). Since the arrangement amounted to a contract of service rather than of tenancy, the magistrate decided in favour of Ndae, and Pretorius was ordered to deliver 100 bags of maize to Ndae's house, as well as to pay Ellenberger's fees. Such cheating by whites was common according to Ndae, but the blacks were generally afraid to sue, and usually did not have access to sympathetic and fearless lawyers like Ellenberger.

But this Pyrrhic victory was also a very costly one. For this episode made a public enemy of Ndae in the eyes of the local white farmers. 'They were so angry that they wanted to kill me by shooting me. . . . They said that I was a spoilt Kaffir to have done that to a white man.' It was directly as a result of the case that Ndae left the Lindley district for good, fearing the consequences of his continuing to stay in the midst of the aroused and angry white community. Many of his relations stayed behind, scattered around the district, mostly as labour tenants much reduced in status and wealth.

The Makumes had managed to maintain their large flocks of sheep by spreading them around the farms on which members of the kin group had settled; but this was a temporary and unsatisfactory expedient – not least because loyalty to the kin group was unlikely to survive once it had effectively broken up. Thus it is not surprising to find Ndae and his young family, together with the young son of one of his uncles who came along as a herd, taking refuge in Lesotho in about 1929 with the family's sheep – 480 at that time, he recalls. This task was entrusted to Ndae, as his father's youngest son. He had been allocated his share of the livestock already; but his brothers were still expected to work for their elders on the farms.

Just as his forefathers had emigrated from Lesotho to seek more land and better conditions on the farms of the South African highveld, so Lesotho was now a refuge for those fleeing the forces of dispossession sweeping across the South African countryside. Ndae settled at Maliba-matso under Chief Mafeketsane. It would seem that the Makumes, like many others on the farms of the Orange Free State, had maintained or resurrected clan affiliations or political allegiances in Lesotho, which could be utilised in times of trouble. But Lesotho, like the black reserves in South Africa, had long ceased to be able to sustain its own population without massive resort to labour migrancy. The opportunities for independent, full-time farming in the villages of the lowlands had long since eroded – except perhaps for the chiefly lineages. Furthermore, the decline of the rural economy in black reserves and territories like Lesotho bore a direct relation to declining opportunities for independent farming by blacks in white-settled rural areas of South Africa.

Ndae did not enjoy his stay in Lesotho. He was not used to having to take pack animals over long distances to sell a bag or two of maize, and having to sleep on the road in the process. He was used to the short trip to the local town on a wagon or cart to offload produce. He did not like the way cattle and donkeys were illtreated, overworked and underfed in Lesotho. He continued paying his tax in South Africa as he realised he could not stay in Lesotho. Furthermore, Ndae soon discovered that his family's livestock was no more likely to survive in Lesotho than on the farms. The sheep population of Lesotho was already very dense. The colonial administration was just then introducing mandatory dipping to combat the disease of 'scab' which was rampant in the emaciated flocks of the Basotho, and which was threatening the sheep of the white farmers of the border districts. White officials from the Orange Free State were deputed to undertake the dipping. Given the inevitable rate of mortality amongst ill-fed sheep, the suspicion quickly spread that the South Africans had been brought in to kill the animals. Ndae still believes this to have been the case.

'They pretended to be improving the quality of our

wool in Lesotho, but everybody soon realised that the real reason for dipping our sheep was to make us bankrupt and very poor, in order to make us dependent on them so that they could take Lesotho from us. That is how clever these people are.'

Before the dipping, many people in Lesotho owned more than a thousand sheep; afterwards there were virtually no sheep or goats left, asserts Ndae, and the people were left destitute. (It needs to be added though that this was at least in part a result of drought and overgrazing – but Ndae's conspiracy theory is not unreasonable if seen in the larger context of his life experiences.) He remembers: 'After that dipping the sheep were so lean that they could not be skinned when they died. When you tried to skin them, the skin would tear off in pieces.'

Ndae lost all his family's many sheep during his unhappy couple of years in Lesotho. But he still remembers one celebrated event with undisguised glee: the day in 1930 when the future king Seiso dipped a 'Boer'. Seiso had set aside ten animals which he had instructed were not to be dipped as they were to be slaughtered for meat. The white official refused to be deflected from his purpose by this royal instruction. On hearing that his orders had been disobeyed, Seiso rode in a rage to the dipping tank. The ensuing argument ended with Seiso pushing the white official into the tank. When the latter was allowed to climb out, he staggered away, fell and died, probably having swallowed some of the toxic dipping compound. Seiso went into hiding with Chief Motsoeneng at Matlakeng, a chief who hated whites, according to Ndae. Motsoeneng dared the administration to come and arrest the refugee, but to come prepared for war. 'He then instructed his men to

28

prepare their guns and be ready to fight.'

But these small, sweet victories against the encroaching tentacles of white domination were inconsequential; and Ndae soon had to join the throngs of his fellow countrymen taking the train to the Witwatersrand gold fields, getting a job as a mine worker in Brakpan. Before that he had not thought of selling his labour; he did not even know where the Witwatersrand was. The year was 1932, and the terrible drought of that year put paid to any hopes that he might recoup his losses in Lesotho. Like all Basotho of his generation, Ndae remembers that drought as 'the great winds of red dust'.

At the mine he made 6 or 8 pounds per month. He made extra money by selling cloth which he bought from a wholesaler in Johannesburg. During this period he lived in the Germiston location known as Dukathole. He worked for a couple of years for a manufacturer of borehole drills in Church Street, Johannesburg, earning 27 shillings per week. Ndae then went to work in Vereeniging for a small building contractor named Terblanche, a quarrelsome man under whom he was to work for eleven years, earning 30 shillings a week to start with. As we shall see, this marked the beginning of an important new chapter in Ndae's life. Meanwhile, his wife and two young children (Miriam and Julia) were living with her parental family, who were still at Doornkloof in the Lindley district.

All this while Ndae was biding his time, awaiting the opportunity to return to farming. Like so many others in his position, he fully intended reaccumulating the resources needed to return to the land, and was determined not to give in to the forces of dispossession. He was soon the owner of a span of sixteen Afrikander calves, paying 5 or 6 pounds per bullock. These he bought at a sale from one Petrus Muller on whose farm, Boskop, between Vereeniging and Heidelberg south of Johannesburg, he settled in the latter half of the 1930s, hoping to rebuild his life as a farmer. At the same time he continued to work for the builder Terblanche in nearby Vereeniging and Vanderbijlpark. On Muller's farm lived Abraham Mokale, as well as one Setlabela and some other Kgatla families like Makani. These had spans of oxen, and were engaged in ploughing on shares and transport riding in the vicinity. Ndae claims that the oppression of the blacks was not as bad in this industrial region as in Lindley district further south in the Orange Free State. There were still opportunities here and there for blacks to prosper in a small way and to live independently.

Indeed, Ndae lived contentedly at Boskop for perhaps sixteen years, farming maize with his Afrikander oxen which he had trained himself, and sharing his crop with his landlord Muller. He built a house on Muller's farm and fetched his wife Anna and children from her parental home at Doornkloof. Her parents were now dead, and her brothers were beginning to suspect Ndae was 'playing a game with them' by leaving Anna in their care. Ndae's daughters Miriam and Julia helped in the fields, even tilling the land with his span of oxen. Ndae would tend his cattle and his fields on his return from work in town in the evenings. No doubt there was also a lot of co-operation between the tenant families. With one span and limited family labour, this was not arable farming of the kind that Ndae had known in the old days. Nevertheless, he did manage a crop of 160 or 170 bags in good years.

Ndae remembers Muller as a kindly and tolerant man. Apparently Muller's farming practices were the cause of

30

much hostility from neighbouring whites who resented the superior and diligent black farmers on his land. But there can be no doubt of the gratitude felt toward him by his black tenants, who managed to escape the axe of dispossession for a few years under his protective patronage. Ndae remembers Muller sitting outside his (Ndae's) house, drinking coffee and eating Ndae's maize porridge, obsessively counting the bags of grain as they came from the threshing machine, in case he be cheated of his half share of the crop. '*Jy gaan my verneuk, ou Jakob*' ['You are going to cheat me, old Jacob'], he would mutter.

Meanwhile, in Terblanche's employ he was developing an interest and a skill in the craft of building. Ndae had realised that there were no long-term prospects on the land for a black man in South Africa, and certainly none for his children. In the light of the alternative opportunities that were to open up for his younger children in later years, Ndae's new career as a builder seems to demonstrate an unusual prescience. For while most of his peers were being sucked into the proletarian vortex of industrial South Africa, Ndae was learning to exploit new and unintended consequences of the economic development of South Africa.

Ndae began in Terblanche's employ as a common worker. But he had other ideas. He was convinced that he could learn building skills himself, and apply them independently. However, the idea of a black man learning how to lay bricks and apply mortar was abhorrent to the white artisans with whom Ndae worked. A racially defined closed shop was strictly applied, and the racial division of labour was enforced by law. Just as independent black commercial farming flew in the face of the ideal of racial supremacy being

31

enshrined in white popular consciousness and in the statute book, so did any form of black entrepreneurial initiative in urban areas threaten the base of the racial order.

But Ndae had spent a good part of his life fighting the forces of dispossession in the countryside, and had learned a thing or two. He had the resourcefulness and insight to know that the white man's law was not so impermeable or impenetrable as the whites liked to think. There were ways in which blacks could survive and even prosper in a hostile environment, and there were opportunities that could be exploited in the nooks and crannies of economic and social life where the white man's law could not reach. Ndae also knew from his experience of Petrus Muller and many others that there were whites who were prepared in practice to flout the formal and informal rules of racial interaction. This was not entirely for selfless reasons; there were profits to be gained by whites at little cost or risk from black tenant production. Similarly, the prohibitions against blacks acquiring skills and against black entrepreneurial initiative raised the expense of, for example, home-building.

So Ndae watched carefully as he went about his work in Terblanche's employ. But he did more than just observe:

'Whenever the whites were having their lunch and talking amongst themselves, I would lay four bricks and paint them just as I had seen my baas do, and I would then run off and sit as if I had done nothing. When the whites resumed work after lunch, I would watch to see if my baas noticed and removed my four bricks, but to my joy he would continue without noticing them. Then I realised that I knew how to build, and I was determined that when I left that contractor I was going to buy

32

building tools for myself and start building.'

The white bricklayer under whose authority Ndae was placed must have had some inkling of this, and was prepared to encourage Ndae's talents – not from humanitarian motives, but because of his own want of diligence. He instructed Ndae to help him by building from the inside when the other whites were not present.

'He told me as soon as the inspectors appear, I must stop and behave like a labourer. He was always in a position to see them from afar as he stood on a trestle. We knew the inspectors by their big cars. . . . You could be arrested if an inspector saw you. But if the owner of the company caught you building he would be very angry with the white builder for allowing Kaffirs to spoil his job. They never caught me building. . . . [The inspectors] would impose a fine on both, the black man and his immediate white baas, who would be fined so heavily that he would never again allow a Kaffir to handle a trowel in his presence. But they could not stop us from learning how to build.'

Again, Ndae knew how to exploit the gap between the law and its implementation, between principle and practice. What white men believed in their collective perceptions often conflicted with their private interests. Ndae was ultimately appointed a foreman over the other black labourers by Terblanche, and now earned the princely sum of £4 18s 6d per week. 'I then went to work with polished shoes and a neat appearance,' recalls Ndae. Terblanche still knew nothing of his ambitions or of his secret accomplishments.

Ndae left Terblanche's employ after the end of the war. He was now able to set up independently as a builder. He bought trestles, wheelbarrows and all the tools required for his trade. He built some outhouses for his landlord Muller; but his first major accomplishment was to build a house for Hendrik van der Merwe on his farm Houtkop on the outskirts of Vereeniging. What brought Ndae to Van der Merwe's attention was, it seems, the latter's reluctance to pay the going rates commonly charged by the recognised white contractors. Ndae, for all his skills, had no legitimacy in the eyes of the law, no contractual standing, no protection against exploitation or deceit. Indeed, when he built Van der Merwe's house, the relationship between them was that between master and servant.

'I did not charge him because he was my master and he could pay me any amount he wanted to pay me. Actually he paid me quite well. He would confidentially ask me to go to his house to get some money. He would always ask me not to tell anybody that he had paid me money. I would then go to his house in secret and he would give me, say, £50, and remind me not to talk about it.'

Ndae was soon building for others in the vicinity, on the farms and in the new industrial towns of Vanderbijlpark and Sasolburg, at rates well below those which white contractors would have charged. His vulnerability, the illegitimacy of his enterprise, was also his strength. He was always dependent on the good will of employers, in strictest confidence, to pay him commensurately with his labours and his skills. There was always the danger of local whites closing ranks against this appalling breach of racial ethics. Van der Merwe had good reason to insist on complete silence on Ndae's part about the true nature of their relationship.

Ndae hired labour to help him, but remembers his workers as an unreliable lot who could not be trusted to turn up to work on Mondays. 'I was always angry with them because I was still expected to pay them.' Nevertheless, Ndae did comparatively well. He says with perhaps a touch of nostalgic exaggeration: 'As soon as I had finished one job, another white was waiting and would rush for me and my tools and trestles and equipment.' Some of his clients, like Albert van der Westhuizen, even wrote testimonials for him. Some whites were clearly less sensitive than others about the opinion of their peers.

Meanwhile, Ndae had continued living on Petrus Muller's farm until Muller died in the mid-1950s. 'A kind man does not live long,' comments Ndae. Again, Ndae discovered that the generational transition bore only ill for the blacks. Muller's son told Ndae that he was not responsible for his father's death: '"I am not going to be like my father to you people." . . . He told me that under his rule, I would never again enjoy what I had enjoyed when his father had still been in control.' Even small gestures like the occasional sheep for meat which had been given them were now out of the question. The younger Muller was unhappy about Ndae's building activities and had 'developed some jealousy', says Ndae. He insisted on having access to Ndae's services before others, even when Ndae was engaged in a building job.

Sharecropping agreements were done away with. The workers on Muller's farm were now paid 2 pounds per month plus rations. Ndae's farming activities came to an end when the new landlord forced him to sell his oxen: 'I sold them whilst they were very lean. I tried to persuade him to allow me to stay there for only that year, but to no avail. . . . He would not allow me to fatten them before I could sell them. He told me that it was none of his business that they were lean.'

Ndae sold his animals at an auction sale for the paltry price of 15 pounds each. His two harrows, three weeders and two double-furrow ploughs were bought by a white farmer. But whereas most black farmers in Ndae's position had no alternative but to accept the inevitability of having to sell their labour as unskilled workers, Ndae had his building enterprise to fall back on.

Ndae and his family moved across the Vaal River to Rooirand near Heilbron, a farm belonging to Hendrik van der Merwe, for whom he had already built a house near Vereeniging. Van der Merwe, on hearing that Ndae was leaving Boskop, invited him to go to Rooirand and build another house there. Ndae took with him his two remaining cows, a few chains, yokes and some other equipment, so that, as he puts it, he could show his young children when they grew up the 'old way of living before things changed'. These were still in his storeroom at Viljoensdrif when we found him there.

Ndae and his family stayed at Rooirand for about nine years. He was now a full-time builder. On his arrival at Van der Merwe's farm there were no buildings there at all. Ndae built not only a farmhouse, but a number of other buildings and even dams. While he practised his building skills, travelling widely through the country-side, his wife worked periodically for Mrs Van der Merwe as a domestic servant. She was given a hundred chickens, the eggs from which she sold in Heilbron. Meanwhile, their family had grown. A son, Isaac, had been born while they were still living on Muller's farm, and another daughter, Elizabeth, two years later. They were surprised to discover that they could still parent children.

But once again, Ndae's building activities raised the ire of a younger generation. Van der Merwe's grandson, a 'little boy' Ndae calls him contemptuously, demanded that Ndae stop building and work on the farm. Ndae responded that this was not what he had agreed to with the 'oubaas', demanded his reference book and left Rooirand. This was in the 1960s. Ndae was also getting fed up with the labour problems involved in his building business, and thinking of retirement.

After leaving the Van der Merwes, Ndae and his *moves* family moved to Viljoensdrif on the Vaal River near Vereeniging, in the employ of the black separatist African Methodist Episcopal Church, of which he had been a member since the 1920s. His job was to look after the corrugated-iron church and serve the local farm community between visits by the minister from Sasolburg, who stayed in Ndae's house on his periodical trips to Viljoensdrif. He was sent there by the Reverend Tantsi, president of the Church, whom Ndae had originally met in Germiston in the early 1930s when they had both been members of the local congregation in the location. Tantsi had become an official of the Church in Bloemfontein, and then took over the Heilbron circuit where Ndae again got to know him during his years at Rooirand. Amongst Ndae's achievements as a builder was the construction of the AME church in the new industrial town of Sasolburg south of the Vaal. His relationship with the Church seems to have grown in his later years, especially after his farming activities had ended in the 1950s, eventually earning a certificate as an evangelist. Perhaps the appeal of the Church is revealed in the fact that Ndae did not regard his affiliation as in any way inconsistent with resort to a traditional diviner when, at Viljoensdrif, one of his cows became ill, owing, he says, to 'evil spirits' sent by an ill-disposed person who was jealous of him.

Ndae was now a man of relatively substantial means –
sufficiently so to provide his younger children and
grandchildren with a good education. The lasting legacy
of Ndae's enterprising spirit must lie in the fact that
Isaac graduated with a B.Sc. degree from the University
of the North at Turfloop, and is teaching at a high school
in Qwa Qwa; his daughter Julia's daughter graduated
with a bachelor's degree in 1984 and her son teaches in a
high school in Sharpeville; and Elizabeth, Ndae's
youngest daughter, teaches in Bethlehem, where her
husband, Simon Tlale, is an inspector of schools. Ndae,
who received no formal education himself and who
taught himself to read the Bible, remembers with
amusement how surprised the white lecturers at Turfloop were to discover that their star pupil's father was a
simple peasant. He proudly asserts that he never allowed
his children to work for any white man while they were
living on the farms. But he still regards his investment in
his children's and grandchildren's education partly as an
investment in his own security in old age. Perhaps
another investment in his old age was the 500 rand he
gave to Miriam's son to pay the deposit on a house in
Sebokeng – the house in which he eventually died.

Ndae lived out his declining years quietly at Viljoensdrif, tending his few cows, and supplying the neighbouring black junior school with milk. He gave his building
equipment to his son-in-law once he could no longer use
it himself after a long illness in his seventies. His wife
Anna died in about 1978. When we visited him, Ndae
showed us his storeroom full of bags of stock feed –
groundnuts, lucerne, barley, beans. He introduced us to
his cows and calves, each with its own name (Stompie,
Vaalmuis, Blommetjie), its individual temperament and
physical characteristics, which Ndae discussed with us as

38

if discussing his own children. Now that he had got over his illness he wanted to draw money from his bank account and buy some Jersey cows from a white man in Edenville. Dairying, mused Ndae, was a profitable business.

But in the end optimism and faith were not enough. The forces of dispossession caught up with Ndae even in the ninth decade of his life. It was perhaps too much to hope that this old man would be left to see out the measure of his days, secure against the rapacity of apartheid's dictates. He was not welcome in South Africa's industrial heartland, surrounded by the factories and mines of Vereeniging, Vanderbijlpark, Sasolburg, Coalbrook. His unimposing church, his humble home, his sheds, his cows, his acre of earth, constituted a 'black spot', and hence an unwanted anomaly in this white man's country. Where was he to go? To Lesotho, he was told, for that was where he had been recruited in the early 1930s for work in the gold mines. Instead, he went to live in Sebokeng with Miriam and his grandson's family. He was dead within the year.

* * *

In many ways Ndae Makume was an exceptional man. But he was also a typical product of a peasant society. He had no formal education, and he worked with his hands all his life. He saw the world simply and graphically. He explained the great events of history during his lifetime in personalised, moral terms, a characteristic of illiterate people. For instance, he explained the downfall of General Hertzog's government in 1939 by telling the story of how Hertzog collected money from the Boers to send to Hitler (Ndae called him 'Hertzog's nephew') in a coffin; but the coffin was opened by some suspicious Englishmen, precipitating Hertzog's demise. As soon as Ndae talked of the larger world of the twentieth century, he revealed the limitations of his perceptions. Nevertheless, he had a strong, vivid memory of the details of his life, as well as a shrewd, if unsophisticated understanding of the historical dynamics of racial domination that shaped his world.

Ndae's life story is in part an admission of defeat. Ndae knew and understood the meaning of the battle of Thaba Bosiu against the Boer commandos in 1868, in which his great-great-grandfather Nkgatha fought. He knew and understood the forces of destruction unleashed by the development of the white man's capitalism. He had no answer but to shrug off the imponderables of life and delight in the small, inconsequential stories which demonstrated his people's refusal to abandon their world willingly. Always they were recounted with a remarkable lack of bitterness or rancour, with no discernible indication of racial hostility, and with a keen eye for human foibles and idiosyncrasies.

But the true significance of the story told here lies in the legacy that Ndae left behind for the generations that succeed him. The transition from peasant to urban middle class in the turning of a generation is forged in ways that are generally unnoticed and unapplauded; but nowhere is there to be found a finer demonstration of the human capacity to understand and exploit great historical forces. Ndae Makume's life remains a lesson in adaptation to defeat, of hope in adversity.

Lucas Nqandela (photo: African Studies Institute)

The Life Story of
Lucas Nqandela

Lucas Nqandela told us the story of his life while sitting
in the sun outside his shabby house in the desolate
resettlement township of Ledig just over the hill from
the vulgar ostentation of the hotel complex, Sun City.
There he sat, all morning, every morning, lazily
watching the dirty children playing in the dust, the
women carrying water from the communal pump or
sticks of wood for cooking the evening meal, the mangy
dogs sleeping in the middle of the rutted dirt road, and
the chickens foraging in the piles of garbage which litter
the treeless landscape. He had to wait there patiently for
his grandchildren to come home from school with the
key to the front door so that he could go inside and
escape the unremitting heat of the midday sun. He was
an old, sick man when we first came across him, already
dying from a chronic heart disease. A less dignified old
age was hard for us to imagine. But behind the decaying
façade we found a keen intelligence, gratified to be able
to talk of the places where he had lived and the people he
had known.

Lucas Nqandela comes from a very different background to that of Ndae Makume. Whereas Ndae was
born into a family group that had not really begun to
experience the insecurities of the twentieth-century

capitalist world – which indeed had not yet reached its pinnacle of prosperity – Lucas was born into a family that was, even before the turn of the century, proletarianised. For Lucas comes from the Ciskei, the area which perhaps more than any other had experienced the social dislocations, the opportunities and the pressures of the colonial economy from quite early in the nineteenth century.

Lucas's African name is Mabuti, but it is perhaps indicative of his family's early circumstances that he has always been known by his European name. Born in 1898, he is of a Mpondo clan, Ngutyana. The original Nqandela, from whom the family derives its surname, was Lucas's great-grandfather. Lucas remembers his father only as Charlie; his mother was Dinah, of the Ntlane family. His parents spoke both English and Afrikaans as well as Xhosa. Lucas does not know much of his parents' families. He was born into a poor, propertyless family, consisting of only his parents and their children. He never knew what it was to live in the large extended homesteads that his forefathers had known in Pondoland further east. They lived in a village in a reserve close to Whittlesea south of Queenstown. Lucas's father worked for a wealthy African notable named Mdingi of the Mbongwa clan. Mdingi exemplifies the extent of economic and social differentiation wrought by generations of intense contact with the trading and farming economy of the Cape Colony. As well as being a wealthy farmer with very considerable herds and flocks and extensive underground storage bins for his grain, he also ran a profitable transport-riding business and owned a number of ox wagons. Mdingi also owned a farm near Queenstown remembered by Lucas as Ndlovukazi, where his sons Khofana and Kholi lived while their father lived in his home at Whittlesea. Lucas's father was a transport rider in Mdingi's employ, driving his spans of oxen.

Lucas's father met with a debilitating accident while transporting grain for Mdingi: his overcoat got caught in the spokes of a wheel, dragging Charlie off the platform and crushing his leg. He never fully recovered and walked with a pronounced limp for the rest of his life. It was as a result of this incident that he left Mdingi's employ, taking his small family to Sterkstroom district further inland, where he entered the employ of a Mr Burns, a sheep farmer, whose son Raymond knew the Nqandelas as a shopkeeper in Whittlesea. Charlie worked as a shepherd, and Lucas remembers as a child helping him chase the lambs when required to do so (although the children received no pay). Burns, who lived with his unmarried son Irvine, owned several hundred sheep, but ploughed only a very limited area for forage. Lucas's mother worked as a domestic servant, scrubbing the floors and doing the washing and ironing. Charlie earned 10 shillings a month plus six or eight jam tins of maize a week, from which his wife made samp for the family's consumption. There was only one other black family on Burns's land, for the large Karoo sheep farms required little labour.

Lucas's parents had four children when they moved to Sterkstroom, the oldest being Agnes, followed by Lucas and his twin brother Motoi, and then Jessie. A fifth child, Sophie, was born on Burns's farm. The quality of life on the sheep farms of the Cape was very depressed, and for a long time the population, both black and white, of the sheep districts had been dwindling. Overgrazing of the Karoo scrub, the engrossing and fencing of farms, meant that economic opportunities were declining. Black workers on the farms who were dependent solely on wage income, and without membership of any larger homestead community in the arable black reserves, were the least privileged and most depressed of the black population.

In about 1910 the Nqandelas met a man named Radebe, a Mosotho who came to Burns's farm as an itinerant sheep shearer. Radebe, who was familiar with the northern Orange Free State and had worked during the maize harvest on the farms at piece-work rates, advised Lucas's father to take his family to the maize districts of the highveld, where, unlike the sheep districts of the eastern Cape, agriculture was booming, opportunities for blacks to prosper were increasing, farms were being subdivided, and propertyless workers were in great demand. So in about 1910 the Nqandela family took the train northward over the Orange River on to the highveld, leaving Lucas's younger sister Jessie behind to work as a household servant for Mdingi, who was now in a wheelchair and needed to be cared for. On the train northwards Lucas encountered Sesotho for the first time; this was a language his mother understood, so she acted as translator in their stuffy third-class coach, filled with migrants travelling to the Witwatersrand gold fields.

The Nqandelas' move northwards was not an isolated decision, but was part of a larger social movement. Opportunities beckoned for the poorer and landless Africans of the eastern Cape; and amongst the farmers of the arable highveld, the African immigrants from the Cape were widely regarded as especially amenable and suitable servants. Whereas wealthier Basotho homesteads gravitated toward farms on which their animals and productive equipment could be accommodated and

46

put to use – in sharecropping relationships as often as not – the poorer immigrants from the Cape were more likely to establish themselves on the land of capitalised white farmers.

Lucas's family settled on Charlie Preller's farm, Doringdraai, near Bothaville in the northern Orange Free State, the farm on which Radebe lived. Others on the farm were all Basotho and Batswana, about seven families in all, including the Cele and Dlamini families. Lucas's father was again employed to look after Preller's sheep, and his young children did odd jobs for their father, although they received no remuneration from Preller. Preller had another farm nearby on which all his arable production was concentrated. Doringdraai was used as a grazing farm, on which Preller's cattle, sheep and horses were kept. Several of the Nqandelas' neighbours worked periodically on Preller's other farm, mostly helping with the cultivation.

As was generally the case where farm employees had no independent productive potential of their own, Preller's tenants had plots of land ploughed for them as payment for their services, on top of a wage of 10 shillings per month. On Preller's farm, as elsewhere in Lucas's experience, these plots amounted to 'three acres', an acre being commonly defined as an area 20 paces wide and 300 long – yielding anything from 5 to 20 bags of maize a year. Of these it was sometimes possible to sell some surplus bags and earn a few pounds. Milk was a rarity in Lucas's young years as they had no cows. This form of remuneration was of particular benefit to employers as it lent some stability to the work force; tenant families had an interest in staying on the farm until the harvest and were unlikely to abscond at some crucial stage in the productive cycle. It also eased the liquidity problems of farmers whose income was irregular and unpredictable, given the nature of agricultural production, and who might have difficulty in meeting a substantial monthly wage bill.

Lucas remembers accompanying the cart pulled by four horses which took Preller's butter to the farm Klipkraal on the road between Kroonstad and Bothaville, where it would be picked up by the post cart carrying the mails and other goods between the two towns. Preller's employees would then return the following day to pick up the empty containers once the butter had been delivered to the storekeepers in Kroonstad. At Klipkraal they would also pick up Preller's mail and any other parcels consigned to him from Kroonstad station. Occasionally Lucas accompanied the horse cart as far as Kroonstad itself, a journey which necessitated an overnight stay in the town as the horses could not do the trip twice on the same day. He remembers the blisters on his hands from cutting fodder for the horses' sustenance.

Amongst Lucas's memories of these early years in the northern Free State was the Boer rebellion which followed the outbreak of the First World War in 1914. Many of the young white men in the district went off to join the armed forces; but many of those staying behind took up arms against the government. 'It was war right here at home,' remembers Lucas. The rebels travelled the countryside, commandeering horses on the farms they passed, including those belonging to black tenants. They also rode their horses through the standing crops of loyalist farmers in order to destroy them, pulled down fences and sabotaged any farm property they came across. 'When they came to a farm house they would first ask, "*Waar is die baas?*" ["Where is the master?"], and we would tell them they were all gone. They then

48

asked us where the horses were and if there were any horses they would simply take them away.'

More alarmingly, bands of rebels were known to carry off young men from black households to act as *achterryers* (grooms) on their campaigns. Lucas remembers a band of these rebels feeding their horses on a stack of reaped wheat which he and other boys were guarding against birds. Lucas and his friends fled into a nearby thicket of bushes to escape being captured. On another occasion he saw a band of rebels galloping across the veld towards him, followed by a detachment of troops. The rebels rode their horses across a flooded river – Lucas thinks some did not make the other side. Eventually, the rebellion ended when the local rebels were forced into hiding on a mountain close to Voorspoed station near Kroonstad. Lucas heard heavy guns being fired at night; and eventually the rebels were forced into submission.

When Preller sold his grazing farm, Lucas's family moved on to the neighbouring farm owned by Frans Naudé, where Charlie continued to work as a shepherd. There Lucas entered the service of a white *bywoner* (or tenant), looking after his sheep and feeding his horses, and also accompanying the bywoner on trips as a groom. The bywoner was poor, and owned only one cow for milking. Lucas was his sole servant, and was paid a sheep a month. At the end of his period in the bywoner's employ, he had accumulated a small flock. He was still an adolescent at this time. Meanwhile, his father's lame leg was making it increasingly difficult for him to perform his functions, and they soon moved on to Dudley Forwood's farm, also between Bothaville and Kroonstad. The Nqandela family had grown by two since their arrival in the Free State; Alfred was born in 1911 and Johannes in 1914. They were on Forwood's farm when the First World War ended and the deadly influenza epidemic of 1918 – known as the '*drie dag*' – hit them. Lucas remembers the influenza well: it was the first time he had seen dead bodies. 'Traditionally as children we were not allowed to go to the graveyard; only adults could go to dig graves and to bury the dead. But that year, although we were still young, we were required to go and assist in digging graves.'

Nobody in his family died, but they buried many people whom they knew.

Lucas's family stayed with Forwood and his son J. C. through the 1920s, although as was common with members of black farm families, Lucas seems to have occasionally entered the employ of other farmers nearby for longer or shorter periods. Forwood was a wealthy English-speaking maize farmer, who had twenty spans of oxen for ploughing. On his farm Lucas began to work full-time to secure his family's tenancy. Like so many other arable farmers, Forwood remunerated his workers by ploughing a small plot for them, as well as paying a monthly wage of 10 shillings and a ration of half a bag of maize meal and salt for making porridge. But here the Nqandelas' harvest was better than they had known previously; they received perhaps 40 bags in good years, enabling them to sell a good surplus at anything from 5 to 12 shillings per bag to the storekeepers in Bothaville.

Although it was now Lucas and his siblings who were working, all their earnings were paid directly to their father who controlled the family's income. Lucas asserts that into his adult life he did not know that wages were paid at the end of the month. He had to approach his father if he required money for any purpose. 'The modern practice of you youngsters doing what you like with your money was unknown to us.' Forwood was not

50

unusual amongst farm employers in seeking to uphold parental authority over even adult children. Unremitting control over the labour and lives of able-bodied young men and women was in the interests both of the farmers and of the older generation in black farm families, for security of tenure in their old age depended on their ability to guarantee the continuing service of their offspring.

Forwood, who was quite elderly, employed white foremen to oversee the activities on the land. Lucas remembers them with little affection. The workers had to rise at three o'clock in the morning, and in the ploughing season the oxen had to be inspanned well before sunrise. Lucas learned to identify each ox so that it could be inspanned in its proper place in the dark by closely scrutinising its horns. The foreman would then arrive, and if the spans were not ready to set to work he would rant at the workers. Lucas remembers the ritual denunciations: *'Jou verdomde skepsel, jy is parmantig, nè? Hoekom kom jy so laat?'* ['You damned creature, you're cheeky, aren't you? Why are you so late?']

Three spans would plough a single field simultaneously, operating in a diagonal line, each third plough with a planter attachment dropping seed and fertiliser into the furrows ploughed by the two spans ahead of it. Lucas considers that fourteen oxen were ideal for ploughing. If more were employed some would not exert themselves and it was difficult for the driver to detect which were guilty of relaxing on the job. A good driver would know in a span of fourteen which were not pulling. While working in the fields, the men would outspan their oxen at midday so that they could go and drink water, while they sat down to a meal of sour porridge, samp or bread brought by their womenfolk. The foreman would occasionally ride over to gaze languidly at what the men were up to, and ask futile and ignorant questions like, '*Hoekom is die ploeg nie gesmeer nie?*' ['Why isn't the plough greased?'] Only on Sunday was there a break from the sapping routine of farm work – except for domestic servants and milkers. On Sundays the Nqande-las would go to the black Methodist church in the vicinity – a denomination which was associated with the more educated and progressive black sharecroppers of the highveld, but which clearly also met the needs of the more lowly of the labouring class to judge by its membership figures of well over 50 000 blacks in the Orange Free State alone.

The harvest season was the busiest time for the farm workers. All available labour – including temporary employees from other farms – was enlisted to break the cobs off the plants and deposit them in piles. Forwood had four ox wagons which were used to carry the maize cobs from the fields after harvest to the steam threshing machine ('those old machines that looked like train engines') which he hired from the contractors who took their threshers around from farm to farm pulled by oxen. Once threshed, the bags of grain had then to be transported to the co-operative society at Amerika railway station north of Kroonstad. The size of For-wood's harvest is indicated by the fact that transporting the crop could take up to three months. They would set out with a loaded wagon late in the afternoon so as to be well-positioned to get to the gates of the co-operative by opening time the next morning ahead of the many other wagons making their way toward the same destination from different directions. They would sleep on the road, and set out before dawn the next day so as to beat the queue which had always formed beside the grain elevators by mid-morning. Lucas proudly relates how his wagon overtook those driven by less experienced or less skilful drivers on the road in the early morning hours. A relay of wagon loads would continue to clear the bags of grain week after week until the crop was eventually disposed of.

The Nqandelas were meanwhile also accumulating some oxen and cows of their own in these years with savings from wages and the sale of grain. Again, all animals were nominally owned by Lucas's father, whoever had bought them. As was generally the case on the farms, Forwood did not allow his black tenants to keep bulls on the farm in order to protect his own cows. Instead they had access to Forwood's bulls. The tenants' animals as well as those belonging to Forwood had free range of the veld and mingled together while grazing.

Nevertheless, Lucas had no illusions about his status as a farm labourer. He knew no other life than as a servant of whites. Unlike so many of the Basotho amongst whom they lived in the northern Free State, his family had long since been fully reconciled to proletarian status. They were quite used to being roundly abused by whites, as they were on Forwood's farm, for wearing their best Sunday clothes and 'pretending' to be equal to whites. Once when he approached a farm house wearing a tie, he recalls with a chuckle, a white girl peered out at him and said, *'O nee ma, is nie 'n mens nie, is 'n kaffir'* ['No, mother, it's nobody, just a kaffir']. When he worked in the vicinity of the farm house, he was given bread and coffee in a jam jar for his lunch at the back door. Even the servants' utensils were not allowed in the kitchen, but hung from a tree in the yard. Friends and relatives visiting the farm during working hours would have to join in the work in progress in the fields if they

53

wanted to avoid being expelled from the farm by the foreman for interfering with the workers.

But the farm workers were not entirely defenceless or cowed. Lucas was still working for the Forwoods when Clements Kadalie's Industrial and Commercial Workers' Union began to organise farm workers in about 1927. Kadalie told them that they were 'wasting their time with the Boers', and that he had bought a large tract of land in Natal for all who wished to leave the farms. His message was not one of rebellion in Lucas's memory, but of total withdrawal from the white man's world. Lucas, like most of the others on the farm, took out member- ship in the Union, paid his fees, and received a membership badge which they pinned to their lapels when whites were not present. They were also prevailed upon to buy copies of Kadalie's booklet for 7 shillings. Only Lucas's twin brother refused to join, saying that he did not want to have anything to do with the whole business. On Sundays Lucas and his fellow members rode into Kroonstad to attend meetings at an open-air bus stop in the black township to hear Kadalie and his lieutenants 'insulting the whites and promising us liberation from their oppression'. He particularly re- members a man named Binda who spoke in Xhosa, Lucas's home language.

But the appeal of the organisation gradually palled when it became clear that Kadalie could not deliver on his promises and when their employers began to threaten them with dire consequences if they continued to attend meetings. They were ordered to destroy their badges and booklets on pain of being beaten. But final disillusion- ment for Lucas came when he saw whites attend the meetings in Kroonstad wearing the white lapel badge of membership; for he began to wonder whether the

54

Union's message was not perhaps a plot by the Boers to impoverish the blacks still further by inducing them to pay money into the organisation's coffers. For how could whites be involved in an organisation that referred to them as 'white pigs', asked Lucas. So when he was ordered to pay membership fees for his invalid father and mother, he refused. 'This is nonsense,' he declared. 'After all, there is actually nothing that Kadalie does for us.' Lucas's considered verdict on Kadalie is that 'he came to rob us in partnership with the whites'. The truth was that the movement's messianic idealism was without any practical usefulness for the workers on the farms. Eventually Kadalie 'just vanished like water vanishing under the ground'.

In the meantime Lucas got married in 1927 to a girl living on Forwood's farm. Furthermore, the Nqandelas were accumulating the means to cultivate the land themselves. The year 1930 found Lucas and his family on the farm Rhenosterhoek next to Voorspoed station north of Kroonstad, hired by one Smulowitz. Smulowitz had no equipment, and used the ploughing spans of his tenants. Lucas and his brothers could plough their own fields once they had finished working on the white man's fields, using their own plough and oxen. This was something of a turning point in Lucas's career on the farms. For the first time he was the master of some of the resources necessary for arable farming, and he was using these to pay for his family's tenancy. In a modest way, he had become a farmer himself, thus once again proving that the usual generalisations about the rise of the white-controlled capitalist farming economy hide a wide diversity of individual experience. But they did not stay at Rhenosterhoek long. Smulowitz seems to have been typical of a particular type of speculator who hired a farm for perhaps a year or two in order to make a quick profit from the farming enterprise of black tenants (usually under sharecropping contracts).

So after the 1930 harvest Lucas and his family moved to Matjiespan south of Viljoenskroon, a farm belonging to Lionel Whitfield, where they were to stay until 1934. Whitfield also used the Nqandelas' span of oxen to supplement his own, while in addition allowing Lucas to cultivate a field for himself and paying him the usual wage of 10 shillings plus a ration of maize meal every week. Others on the farm, such as Las Makibidi and Moswetsa, also owned spans which were used on Whitfield's lands as a condition of their tenancies. Many different black families lived on Matjiespan and on the neighbouring farm Windsor, also owned by Whitfield, but only some of them owned ploughing spans. Lucas remembers that Whitfield would arrive in his motor car well before dawn every morning in the ploughing season and would sit in the car with the headlights on so that the workers could see what they were doing while inspanning the oxen. Nine spans were used simultaneously to plough Whitfield's lands.

Lucas's family was still together on Matjiespan, still nominally under his father's authority, although old Charlie was now unable to work. Lucas's first-born son, Jeremiah, born in 1929, died in infancy. Another son, Edwin, was born on Smulowitz's farm, and was followed by their first daughter Vuyelwa, born on Matjiespan in 1932. Lucas's twin brother was now married too. They were also joined there by Lucas's wife's elder sister's family. His brother-in-law, Albert Matiwane, owned no oxen, but had three acres ploughed for him by Whitfield as was usual for propertyless workers. Matiwane's job on the farm was to drive the tractor which Whitfield bought

56

– perhaps as a result of the devastating drought of 1932 which killed large numbers of oxen.

While working on Whitfield's farm it was brought home to Lucas that black-owned stock on white land survived on sufferance and was especially vulnerable to the vagaries not only of the climate, but of the white man's enterprise as well. For, unlike other farmers for whom Lucas had worked in the past, Whitfield insisted on segregating his animals from those of his black tenants. He had fenced his land into grazing camps, and the fresh, sweet veld, left to grow undisturbed through the summer, was reserved for his livestock alone. The blacks could only use those camps which had already been exhausted by their employer's cattle. The consequence was that in the great drought of 1932, one of the reference points in the lives of all who lived through it, Lucas's family lost thirteen head of cattle and a horse. Scarce fodder was railed in, and Whitfield jealously refused to sell any of it to his tenants. 'He told me pointedly that he could not afford to starve his cattle in favour of mine,' recalls Lucas.

In the following year, 1933, the Nqandelas' crop failed, and Lucas bought seven bags of maize on credit from a white trader to feed his ageing parents. The following year the yield was very good, and Lucas tried to repay the seven bags. But the price of maize had plummeted from the high of the previous year to a mere 4 shillings per bag. '*Jy is mal. Ek soek my geld*' ['You are mad. I want my money'], said the storekeeper. So Lucas had to pay back the money value of the maize at the inflated levels ruling in the previous year. Nevertheless, the Nqandelas' big crop of 1934 (Lucas says it was some 150 bags – the biggest they had ever known by a long way) enabled them to re-establish their independence fairly rapidly, despite the losses caused by the drought.

So in 1934 Lucas took the decision to leave the Orange Free State and move to the western Transvaal, where the opportunities for some degree of independent farming seemed greater than in the faster-developing capitalist economy of the rural Free State. At this point Lucas split from his twin brother who stayed behind, and moved northward to Frederikstad, on the railway line northeast of Potchefstroom, together with his brother-in-law Albert Matiwane. The farm was owned by one Kowolik who lived in Johannesburg and visited the farm occasionally. Living on the farm were a couple of Afrikaans foremen, Steyn and Schoeman, who appear to have been little more than bywoners, whose job it was to watch over the activities of the black tenants. The conditions of tenancy were formalised here in the very common convention of 'four days/two days' – four days of work in the landlord's fields and two days in their own fields – but using their own ploughing spans and equipment and family-based labour organisation.

This convention and others like it were not dissimilar to the more explicit sharecropping relationships still to be found on the farms, insofar as the white landholder's profits depended on black productive resources and black productive enterprise. But the separation of fields and the separation of labour time (rather than simply the separation of the yield after threshing as was the case in sharecropping arrangements) made for a far less equal relationship than did pure sharecropping. For white landholders could reserve for themselves the best and most fertile lands, and give the tenants lands which were virgin and thus took much longer to plough or which were already worn out through successive years' use. White landholders could also reserve for themselves

58

improved seed or fertiliser issued by the co-operative society on credit. For these same reasons, such relationships were less likely to raise the ire of the surrounding white community as were explicit sharecropping relationships, where no supervision at all was required until the reaping and threshing to guard against cheating by tenants. In contrast, the nature of the arrangement on Kowolik's land presupposed a high degree of supervision during the four days a week when the tenants were working on the landlord's lands, to ensure that the work was done (after all, the tenants had no direct interest in the landlord's yield). Hence the intrusive presence of Kowolik's 'foremen'.

Kowolik was typical of many an urban-based, speculative landholder, often Jewish, who owned or hired land with a view to making a profit from black tenant production. Lucas's instincts were sound when he moved north of the Vaal, for in the districts around the industrial and mining centres of the southern Transvaal much farm land was used for these purposes, with corresponding opportunities for black farmers seeking to escape the proletarian vortex. There was no limit to the extent of land Lucas and his brother-in-law could plough for themselves. The four months from August to December were devoted exclusively to ploughing for the summer maize crop.

'We used to plough as much as we could manage. As long as there was still space, and as long as we were also ploughing for him, he could not be bothered how much land we ploughed. We used to do everything on his farm; all the responsibility was ours.'

The fact that no wage, in cash or kind, was paid to the tenants on Kowolik's land served as a tacit confirmation that Lucas and his fellow tenants were not servants, but independent producers paying rent from the produce of the soil. However, they did expect to be paid if they were asked to plough on another farm further north, which required them to leave their own fields for longer than the stipulated four days a week. So when the foreman insisted they plough *binnelands* (further in the interior) without payment they moved off Kowolik's farm in 1937. It was while at Frederikstad that old Charlie, Lucas's father, died in 1936. Now Lucas's livestock was his in name as well as in practice.

From Frederikstad Lucas and his brother-in-law Albert and their families moved for a short while on to Doornkloof, a farm belonging to (or leased by) D. Bloomberg, a lawyer living in Johannesburg. By now they had been joined by Joel Dintsi, another brother-in-law married to Lucas's sister. Clearly these family connections were important in combining resources and sharing labour, thereby increasing their joint potential for survival in an insecure and unpredictable world. The arrangements on Bloomberg's farm were not dissimilar to those at Frederikstad; but Bloomberg's farm was a good deal smaller and hence the ploughing land available to the black tenants was limited, so the tenants were paid 3 pounds a month for the use of their ploughing spans and labour during the ploughing season. Moreover and more important, grazing was at a premium at Doornkloof. Lucas and his fellows were given a small grazing camp for their animals. When they complained that it was inadequate, they were told that only their plough oxen could be accommodated, and there was no room for their cows. Bloomberg explained that if a man took a wife, he did not expect to have to support her sister as well. Rather than sell their cows as Bloomberg ordered, they moved off in the winter of 1938.

From there they moved to Cordoville, a farm belong- *move*
ing to Dries Oosthuizen between Fochville and Evaton,
again well within the industrial heartland of South
Africa. Here they stayed from 1938 until 1945, sharecropping with their landlord. Although their yields were
never very large, this was the high point of Lucas's life as
a farmer. With Joel Dintsi (Albert Matiwane left them
after they arrived there) Lucas ploughed and cultivated
the land and reaped the crop with minimal interference
from Oosthuizen. They turned as much land as they
could manage and were responsible for every phase of
the production process until the threshing. Insofar as
their efforts were directed to their own profit as much as
their landlord's, the latter felt no need to keep a close
watch on them, and they were left alone to pursue their
enterprise for the most part. But after the harvest, the
crop was transported by wagon to Oosthuizen's homestead, where it was threshed by a machine hired by and
paid for by the landlord. It was at this stage that
Oosthuizen took charge, for it was at this stage that the
possibility arose of deceit and conflict about the size of
the crop and the size of the landlord's share. Oosthuizen *cheated*
ensured that he received his 50 per cent of the crop;
while Lucas and Joel, who had collaborated in its
production, split the remaining half between them.

Again, the ambiguities of racial dominance on the land
are here evident; for Oosthuizen was no urban-based
speculator, but a resident landowner and farmer and a
member of the local Afrikaans-speaking white community who undoubtedly subscribed to the prevailing social
ideal of white supremacy. Not for the first time are we
confronted by the incongruity that in practice economic
relationships across the colour line often obeyed a
different set of imperatives from those allowed for in the

dominant ideological perceptions of whites.

But this situation did not last. The forces of dispossession were closing in all the time. The year 1945 was the last year Lucas farmed the land. The Second World War had been a politicising experience for Afrikaners, who were again responding to the clarion calls of nationalism. It was not surprising that under these circumstances, as had happened in earlier decades in the Orange Free State, the boundaries of freedom for blacks on the land were narrowing rapidly. Furthermore, tractors were revolutionising the technology of arable production, particularly in the 1940s. The old means of production were becoming obsolete. Draught oxen were no longer needed or wanted. Black family labour was being displaced by the labour of the work gang. Lucas and his family were experiencing the start of a new wave of dispossession and displacement which was to grow in intensity after the National Party came to power in 1948 and which was not to let up even when it encountered the most secure of the blacks on the land, those with freehold rights dating back to before 1913.

Thus in 1945 Lucas and his family moved to Lawley Estates, a smallholding area close to Lenz military base southwest of Soweto, where they went to live on the plot of Alfred Sampson. They now had six surviving children, four of whom were boys, although Sipho, a boy of about 9, was to die shortly. The oldest, Edwin, was now 15. Two more girls were to be born at Lawley, Nonkaizane and Agnes. There Lucas and his wife returned to the life of waged employment from which they had escaped for a few years in the middle of their lives. Lucas's wife did the washing and cleaning for the Sampsons on Mondays to pay for their lodgings, and worked as a domestic for other whites in the neighbourhood for the rest of the week. Lucas got a job from one Grevenhout on the neighbouring farm Elandsfontein, looking after his cattle and working in the dairy. Like his father before him, Lucas's working life was severely impaired by an injury sustained while on the job. He crushed his hand while working with a machine in the dairy, and spent five months in Baragwanath Hospital. Eventually in 1958, after living with the Sampsons for thirteen years, they moved to a black farm near Boons station south of Rustenburg as tenants, where Lucas managed to earn some money by selling wool from his small flock of sheep.

But the state soon caught up with them, and in the early 1960s they, along with all the other residents, were resettled inside the borders of the nearby Pilanesberg reserve, part of the later nominally independent Bophuthatswana. There Lucas lived for another two decades in the barren township of Ledig with his youngest daughter Agnes after his wife died, dependent on his small pension from the state and his daughter's wages. From the dusty, desolate landscape of Ledig, a rusty scrapyard of forgotten humanity, it is difficult to imagine that directly over the hill, a short mile away, lies the glittering pleasure palace of Sun City, where white South Africans – and Bantustan notables – spend their wealth in as extravagant a display of conspicuous consumption as can be found anywhere in the world.

Lucas's children are scattered around the industrial townships of the Witwatersrand and the Vaal Triangle. They all received far more education than their father, who never went to school but was taught to read the Bible by his teenage grandson in Ledig when already an old man. But none of them has managed to escape being sucked into South Africa's industrial proletariat. Thus in a sense, Lucas's success in establishing a modest independent productive base on the highveld farms in adult life was also his weakness. For unlike Ndae Makume, his accomplishments held out no long-term potential for social mobility amongst his children and grandchildren. Nevertheless, the story of Lucas's life again demonstrates the possibilities of exploiting the potential for survival in a small and insecure way in the heart of industrial South Africa throughout the first half of the century, without recourse to the sale of one's labour. But in the long term the forces of dispossession were not to be denied.

Barney Ngakane (photo: SAIRR)

The Life Story of
Barney Ngakane

Barney Ngakane was a tall, erect, proud man who had seen much in his 80-odd years. He was clearly a man of intellectual stature and learning, who spoke English in clipped, precise, decided accents, slowly evaluating each question and choosing his words with care. He lived in a simple house in the dusty thornveld of Bophuthatswana when we interviewed him, in the midst of the mono-tonous Bantustan landscape, dotted with the small, indistinguishable dwellings of families uprooted and turned off land on which they no longer were allowed to live. Farming there is a privilege of the few, and the rest, their menfolk working far away in Rustenburg or Carle-tonville, looked to him as their champion and their adviser in their dealings with magistrate and chief. This

I am grateful to the Archives Department of the South African Institute of Race Relations for allowing me to make use of their interviews with Barney Ngakane, published in mimeo form in their Oral History Series as *A Community Man: An Oral History of the Life of William Barney Ngakane.* Our own interviews with Barney took place a couple of years later, and although we covered the same ground and found out a lot more about the rural dimensions of his life story, he had lost some of his story-telling fluency in the intervening years; so I have tended to make use of the SAIRR transcripts when quoting directly.

67

thankless task he had taken on uncomplainingly; it was a role to which a lifetime of service had well fitted him. It became only slowly apparent that he had known, indeed been on intimate terms with, many leading lights in the history both of African nationalism and of white liberalism in South Africa, and had witnessed more history in the making than most mortals manage in a lifetime. But our main interest was in the rural environment from which the young Barney Ngakane emerged into adulthood, in the social origins which shaped him and, by extension, the whole remarkable class of black South Africans which he represents.

As far back as family memory goes, the Ngakanes lived in the vicinity of what became Vereeniging on the southern side of the Witwatersrand, near the banks of the Klip River. Originally of the Bapogole division of the Bafokeng clan, they had been displaced by the ravages of the Difaqane wars in the early decades of the nineteenth century; and like so many other Sotho–Tswana in the interior highveld region of South Africa, they had become integral, if subordinate, members of the new society developing on either side of the Vaal River in the wake of the great expansion of Boer settlement in the 1830s and 1840s.

Barney's grandfather, Tshaoli, or Wildebees as he was known to the Boers, was a man of some local prominence, it seems, and the mountains on the southern edge of the Witwatersrand were at one time apparently named after him by the locals. A man with some three wives, he was patriarch over a considerable village community on a farm belonging to one Org Marais. It was there that Barney's father Marcus was born, perhaps around 1870 (he was an adolescent when the diggers began to pour onto the Witwatersrand in the late 1880s). Marcus was a child of Tshaoli's youngest wife, a Ndebele woman, and his father was no longer a young man when he was born. The younger members of the kin group worked for the landlord and lived close to the farmstead during their service period, in the usual way. Marcus worked as a herd from a young age.

Barney tells a story of his grandfather that reveals something of the agrarian paternalism of Boer society, and of the social perceptions of the *oorlams* class of African clients within the Boer economy. The old man was a trusted *achterryer* (or groom) who accompanied Boer commandos in their raids and assaults on independent black chiefdoms, and was accorded the privilege, regarded apparently as a great honour, of owning a gun. He was indeed a 'personal friend' of President Paul Kruger himself, Barney tells us. He remembers vividly the story of the day that Paul Kruger's train came through Vereeniging station. His grandfather was there to greet the old president, and when he stepped forward on the platform the assembled Boer notables shouted, '*Keer daar, Kaffir, keer daar!*' ['Stop there, Kaffir, stop there!']; but Tshaoli Ngakane, known as 'Wildebees' to the Boers, turned and asked, '*Waar was julle toe Paul Kruger en ek die land skoongemaak het?*' ['Where were you when Paul Kruger and I cleared the country?']. The president thereupon fetched a gold coin from his pocket and handed it to Wildebees in remembrance of past comradeship in arms.

This story, elaborated perhaps although probably not entirely apocryphal, reveals a belief in a golden age of personal commitment and loyalty, of paternalism and clientship, which has in the popular conception been lost. And to people like the Ngakanes, it is the destruction of that imagined golden age by the forces of

69

greed and dispossession that has provided partial rationalisation for their resistance to the dictates of the white-supremacist state in the twentieth century. This theme in the ideology of resistance might resonate particularly with the experiences of people of Barney's generation and his social and geographical origins; for he was typical of those who experienced both the optimism of the first generation of African improvers and accumulators on the highveld, and the disillusion of the later generations, as we shall see.

Some time before the turn of the century, the community moved further west into the Potchefstroom district after Tshaoli's eldest son Gabriel, who was the wagon driver on the farm, had one day been tied to the wheels of a wagon and beaten for some misdemeanour. Boer paternalism was always leavened by occasional resort to the sanction of violence as a way of asserting dominance. As a result Gabriel had gone off and found another farm on which they could settle, and the entire community absconded overnight with all their possessions, wagon, livestock and all. At some stage they returned to Vereeniging, where they settled on the outskirts of the town, on land owned by the Lewis and Marks partnership. Isaac Lewis and Samuel Marks had begun in about 1879 to exploit the considerable coal resources of the mid-Vaal region, at first for sale to the Griqualand West diamond fields, and had succeeded in accumulating a massive block of land on either side of the Vaal River, comprising almost two dozen farms – known as the Vereeniging Estates.

Black sharecropping tenancy was a profitable concern for the proprietors of these farms, and large quantities of grain were produced by the black farmers to feed the new urban population and the mine compounds. The

Ngakanes were undoubtedly typical of the sort of families, long part of the white-dominated political economy of the highveld, long exposed to commercial values, who were attracted to the potential for profit and self-improvement that sharecropping implied. Share-cropping – farming-on-the-halves – meant a much closer involvement in the world of cash and markets than the clientage relationships that had characterised their lives on Org Marais's farm at an earlier date. The world was changing rapidly as an enclave of advanced industrial capitalism arose in the heart of the highveld, and blacks like the Ngakanes were well-placed to respond to the challenges and opportunities. They participated fully in the accumulative dynamic of the time.

The farm on which the Ngakanes were settled was used during the Anglo–Boer War by the British as an African refugee camp. This was one of a chain of concentrated agricultural settlements set up for blacks along the railway lines, whose purpose was to clear the farms of non-combatants. Many tens of thousands of Africans lived in these camps for the duration of the war; and many died from the epidemic diseases which periodically swept through them. Despite the insecurities of life, for many the high demand and high prices for grain crops, and the opportunities for earning high wages in the employ of the British army as transport workers, guards, scouts or labourers, brought unprecedented financial reward. Nevertheless, by the end of the war the productive resources of Africans in the camps were as often as not decimated. Livestock had not well survived the devastation of the rural areas and the shortage of pasture in the vicinity of the camps, and many black families returned to the farms on which they had lived prior to the war without the means to restart their small-scale family farming enterprises. Old people who remember life in the camps describe them as not dissimilar to life in a modern urban township. The experience must have been a dramatic one in the lives of those who went through them, an experience that has never really been documented, unlike the equally traumatic camps in which so many Boer women and children perished.

It was in the refugee camp, shortly after the war had ended, that Barney Ngakane was born, on 29 December 1902. As the other inhabitants of the camp were slowly repatriated to their old homes, with rations to help them survive the harsh post-war drought, the Ngakanes stayed behind and tried to rebuild their lives as best they could. Barney's grandfather was now dead and the family community was fragmenting. Barney's father Marcus and the latter's brothers, together with a couple of brothers-in-law, continued as sharecropping tenants of the Vereeniging Estates Company. Undoubtedly the support system of the kin group contributed to the black sharecroppers' economic rehabilitation. The poorer whites on the other hand – especially the landless bywoners – often found themselves unwelcome on the farms on which they had previously lived because of their impoverished and dependent state. Wealthier landlords like the Vereeniging Estates, with their experience of the productivity, resilience and self-sufficiency of the black farmers, were also prepared to invest in their tenants by providing them with loans for restocking after the war. Very probably, the Ngakanes had access to such facilities.

But like other landholders with substantial capital resources (individual industrialists, financiers and merchants as well as corporate landowners) the Vereeniging

Estates Company could not resist the temptation to capitalise their production on some of their land as an experiment – once the post-war drought had lifted and financial conditions had improved. In 1907 and 1908 they imported, at enormous expense, steam traction engines from England for ploughing. As a consequence the Ngakanes were obliged to move off in search of alternative land. But the company would have been justified in regretting the departure of their tenants. As was so often the case, capital-intensive production proved financially disastrous. Capital investment did not guarantee corresponding profits. Given the enormous risks involved in arable production (drought, infestation, locusts) and the unresponsiveness of yields to technological innovation, higher costs could simply mean larger losses. The capitalists were learning that, given the technology available at the time, black sharecropping enterprise was quite simply more profitable than capitalised production. For the white landholder, black tenant farming was far less costly and therefore less risky, and probably more productive too (because of the commitment of the tenant family to its own enterprise) than trying to establish direct control over production on their land.

Less wealthy and more practical white landholders already knew this. Indeed, for men like Fanie Cronje on his very substantial farm Vlakplaas some twenty miles to the west of Vereeniging, survival on the land depended on the enterprise of black sharecroppers. The Ngakanes – seven separate households of them now – settled on Vlakplaas after they had been displaced from the Vereeniging Estates, and they were to stay there until 1920. Barney's father Marcus, the latter's brothers – Paulus, Elias, Alpheus, William, Gabriel – and two cousins, Elias and Johannes Nape (Barney's grand-father's sister's sons), and their respective families farmed there individually.

Amongst sharecroppers like the Ngakanes, the extended kin group had ceased to be the primary economic unit. Although their family networks continued to be crucially important to their success as farmers, the primary unit of production amongst the sharecroppers was the individual household. The sharecropping tenants who dominated the economy of the region by the turn of the century entered contracts as individual heads of households rather than as extended communities. Elderly patriarchs such as Barney's grandfather were important agents in the control and direction of the kin group's labour resources in the more land-extensive and less commercialised rural economy of an earlier date. However they played a less and less prominent role on the highveld of the early twentieth century (although, as we saw in the case of the Makumes, they did still exist); and they certainly served little useful function in the more atomised, peasantised economy of the sharecroppers.

A revolution in social and economic organisation had taken place. The authority of seniors had effectively been displaced; and the individual household was now an independent economic unit. Barney Ngakane's earlier years were thus spent in a very different family environment from, say, that of Ndae Makume. Barney's family was essentially a nuclear family, pursuing their individual enterprise, albeit in collaboration with other neighbouring families to whom they were related by blood or marriage.

The Ngakanes were influenced by mission Christianity quite early on. Barney recalls the story about a friend

74

of his grandfather's who threatened approaching evangelists with a spear, but who succumbed to their ministrations when they insisted on singing hymns outside his front door. Tshaoli was not himself a Christian, being a polygamist; but he did encourage his children to pursue an education. Some of Barney's father's generation had learnt a proficiency in English from their Mosotho teacher on the farm. This teacher, Barney thinks, was employed by his grandfather much as Boer notables employed tutors for their own children. He remembers the story of his aunt accompanying the old man into Vereeniging during the Anglo–Boer War so that she could communicate on his behalf with the English officials there.

Both Barney's parents were baptised into the Methodist Church in early adulthood (after marriage, Barney thinks) by the Reverend Mr Sigo, the first ordained black Methodist minister in the Transvaal, who was stationed at Potchefstroom. Methodism seems to have been the church with most resonance for the aspirant commercial farmers, with rather more individualistic and accumulative preconceptions than their forebears. It seems quite likely that the youngest members of the family – like Barney's father – were more free to embrace Christian values – above all, education – than their elder siblings, particularly the offspring of more senior wives. It seems to have been often the case that older children in polygamous families were more closely controlled by their seniors, and were obliged to serve the interests of the kin group or lineage first and foremost – often in earlier days contracting polygamous marriages themselves (although polygyny was unusual on the farms by the early twentieth century).

It was in keeping with this pattern that the last-born in

Tshaoli Ngakane's family (again, like Barney's father) were the most susceptible to new ideas and social and economic innovation. Barney repeatedly stresses his father's unshakeable faith in self-improvement through education. It was Marcus's unfulfilled ambition to go to Lesotho, where educational opportunities were thought to be superior to those available elsewhere. Many extended kin groups from north of the Vaal, their larger communities disrupted by the Difaqane, had made their way into Moshoeshoe's kingdom in earlier years, and many of the sharecropping families in the mid-Vaal region had at some time lived in Lesotho where they had first encountered Christianity as a social and economic force. By Marcus's day, however, Lesotho had been much reduced in extent, and was already showing signs of overcrowding and falling crop yields. By the turn of the century there was no arable land that was not already colonised and cultivated, and Marcus could never realise his wish to take his family to Lesotho. There was, however, a great deal of land available in the heart of the arable highveld on which productive families were welcomed as sharecropping tenants.

On Fanie Cronje's farm Vlakplaas, these cultural imperatives played their role in founding the new community. Barney's father was the driving force behind the establishment of a small school on the farm. The tenants built it themselves with their own labour and materials; they made the benches; and they asked the Methodist Church to provide them with a teacher. The teacher, Eliphas Mashabani, came from Lourenço Marques, according to Barney, and had trained at the Methodists' Kilnerton Institute near Pretoria. He is remembered by Barney as extremely diligent. Young Barney and his contemporaries would rise early enough to be in school at six o'clock in the morning, so that when the younger children arrived at nine, they could help them with their lessons. This level of commitment to education was fundamentally related to a commitment to Christianity, but Christianity of a particular kind: a universalist, inclusive, improving Christianity. Barney tells us that his father did not want him to spend his life farming, but looked forward to a future free of manual toil for his son. However, this cultural optimism was soon shaken, for the Ngakanes as for countless others of their class and their social assumptions at this time.

Indeed, from a young age Barney was aware that despite the central, even dominant, position held by the black farmers in the rural economy of the region, they were politically a subordinate people. Blacks were constantly being reminded of their status as a subject race. Nothing symbolised white authority more insistently than the pass laws, designed in part as instruments of control over the mobility and therefore the bargaining strength of blacks caught in servile relationships. The pass laws also provided whites who had reason to feel threatened by black enterprise with a weapon that could be used to assert their mastery over individual blacks. For others, they were rather more nakedly a means of extortion. Barney remembers the day when his father's plough broke while he was working in the fields, and his father cycled into town to buy a spare part. 'And when he got there, he was arrested for not having a pass; he should have got his landlord to give him a pass to go there. So he said to the policeman, "Look, I am working, have we got time to be looking for passes? So if you want money what is the fine?"'

He handed over the money (extra cash was apparently commonly carried to meet just such an eventuality) and went about his business. There can be little doubt (indeed it was well-known at the time to be the case) that policemen widely exploited the opportunities to earn a private income in this fashion. The structures of racial control have always nurtured corruption. And it was not only officers of the law who were able to benefit informally from the pass laws. Barney recalls of his youth:

'When you travelled from one farm to the next you had to get, to carry a special pass. It meant that if you were going to a farm, or a village, about a mile away, just on the other side of the border of the farm, and the "boss" was seven or eight miles away, you had first to go to him in order to get a pass to get to the other village. Yes, and the farmers exploited this. Whenever an African came along the road they would call to him: "Come here. Where do you come from? Who is your boss? Will you come and chop some wood for me?" And you did that and he let you go. That was the sort of thing that happened.'

People like the Ngakanes, thus, were in a very ambiguous position. A rising rural elite of a sort, determined to use every opportunity to improve their lot within the colonial nexus, they were also in many ways the victims of the dominant culture of racial supremacy, and the experience of rejection was growing in scope and ferocity, as they were soon to discover. Included yet also excluded, they lived life on a razor's edge.

But it was on Cronje's farm in the years from about 1908, when the experience of rejection was becoming everywhere more evident, that the Ngakanes reached the pinnacle of their economic achievements. It was there too that Barney became really aware of his surroundings. It was there that he began to work in the family fields.

Before the move to Vlakplaas, Barney had accompanied the older boys occasionally when herding, but he was still very young at the time. Vlakplaas was divided into camps; so herding was no longer necessary. Barney remembers at age 10 or 12 assisting with the ploughing. The sharecropping families were independent of any direct supervision, and were responsible for organising their own production and meeting all the costs. Unlike most sharecroppers on the highveld, the families on Vlakplaas paid only a third of their crop to their landlord. It was usual to divide crops in halves; occasionally two-thirds were handed over to the landlord when the latter provided some of the resources necessary for producing the crop (beyond the land itself), by way perhaps of a loan or the use of plough oxen. But the Vlakplaas community's extraordinary productivity undoubtedly accounted for the fact that they were able to keep two-thirds of the crop for themselves. Barney claims that each of the seven families produced between 800 and 1 000 muid bags of grain a year – sometimes more. This figure has been corroborated by another Ngakane, a cousin of Barney's, interviewed separately. The major crop was maize, and sorghum was also grown to a lesser extent. Very few black farmers in the southern Transvaal could compete with them, says Barney.

Each family had at least two spans of oxen (fourteen animals were used in a span), double-furrow ploughs, planters and cultivators. Barney does not remember his father ever taking out loans or using a bank – blacks were excluded from such facilities it seems. But, not atypically, their landlord helped them to buy implements and tools by arranging credit with the dealers in Vereeniging. This was done quite informally, and the tenants would then go and fetch what they needed and pay their debts off after harvest.

Women did not work in the fields until the harvest season, when all available labour was called upon to pick the cobs, and load them onto the wagons, from where they were taken to the threshing area close to their homes. Harvest lasted from mid-April through to July, without let-up. The individual families would harvest their own crops initially, and those who finished first would then go and help the others until all available labour in the community converged on the fields of the last family to clear their crops. Wage labour was used to supplement family labour; Barney's father usually had a couple of men from Evaton location helping him, and they would take home thirty or forty bags of maize after threshing as payment for their work.

Threshing operations were performed communally. Steam threshers were making an appearance in the district in the years prior to the First World War, and were owned by individual entrepreneurs or syndicates. They were hired out to the farmers and travelled from farm to farm. It was part of the informal exercise of racial hegemony that only whites could secure the services of the threshing contractors, so the landlord Cronje was responsible for making these arrangements, but it was the tenants who paid the threshing costs of 4 pence per bag threshed. Each family's crop was threshed and bagged in turn, and each family paid for its own crop.

The sharing of the crop constituted almost a ritual, with Cronje himself presiding. This was the one time of the year when the landlord decisively intruded in the productive realm of his tenants. For he wished to ensure that he received what was due to him, and hence he had to count every one of the thousands of bags filled by the threshing machine. One year Cronje asked the black teacher at the farm school (of which more later) to provide him with a bright pupil to help him count, and thereafter the landlord asked every year for the *klein Engelsman* (little Englishman), as he called Barney on account of the impeccable English he had learnt at school, to accompany him as he counted and divided the bags.

Each family had its own ox wagon; and clearing the crop took weeks of hard work. It was part of the contract of tenancy that the tenants had to convey Cronje's share of the crop too – some to his farmstead, the bulk to the Vereeniging Milling Company's premises in town. The milling company bought tenants' as well as the landlord's crops, their sorghum as well as their maize. Barney's father kept back part of his crop for sale in December when prices were higher as supplies began to dwindle, holding, in Barney's memory, as many bags as he could safely store. It seems to have been quite unusual at this time for farmers – black or white – to be able to hold back part of the crop in this way, given the illiquidity of the rural economy and the producer's dependence on the storekeeper's credit during the long months when the farming enterprise was generating little income. Again, the degree of manoeuvrability that these sharecroppers appear to have enjoyed in this respect indicates their relatively privileged position.

Butter-making was also an important activity amongst the tenant community, and was the province of the women. The families owned many milk cows, and they sold a lot of butter in Vereeniging. This enterprise brought in a steady flow of cash to the households, but it is not clear whether the women controlled the income thus generated, or whether it was taken over by their menfolk; the role of women amongst the sharecroppers was undoubtedly a subservient one. Barney remembers one of the duties of the school-going children in the early morning was to milk the cows and drive them to the camps; and after school in the afternoon they would fetch them again. African women from poor labour-tenant families on neighbouring farms would sometimes come over to help work the churns to make butter in the mornings, and would carry off containers of milk as payment. Apart from their herds, the Ngakanes also kept goats and particularly pigs of an uncommonly large breed, which were fed on maize husks; and in winter these were sold to white farmers, often in exchange for a heifer each.

Nobody in the tenant families was expected to work for their landlord, not even the womenfolk, although some of them, including Barney's mother, did laundry work for some of the white families in the vicinity. Very occasionally the tenants would help Cronje out with some special task. Barney recalls once getting up earlier to help drive cattle from Cronje's grazing land into the maize lands after harvesting was complete (access to the standing maize stalks for grazing by the landlord's stock was commonly a condition of tenancy). Moreover, nobody in any of the black households ever left the farm to find wage employment elsewhere. Barney is quite emphatic about that. This was probably a very unusual situation, for one of the strengths of the better-educated sharecropping elite in the region as a whole was their more privileged access to wage income – on the basis of which they were able very often to sustain larger-scale farming enterprises than the mass of rural Africans. To be in a position to avoid wage employment altogether – even by younger dependants in the household – was an index of the Ngakanes' success as farmers. Indeed, they seem to have looked down on urban life. Barney was taught that the rural environment was infinitely healthier than and superior to the towns. 'We looked down on the people who lived at Evaton just next to us,' laughs Barney.

There was inevitably a considerable degree of stratification among blacks on the land – differences in material prosperity and educational expectations and opportunities, as well perhaps in class consciousness. Barney remembers the labour tenants on other farms in the district, some of whom sent their children to the black school on Vlakplaas. Nevertheless, the Ngakanes' commitment to education and to a particular improving brand of Christianity seems to have marked them off quite sharply from other Africans whom they knew in the neighbourhood. Although they got on well with other farm Africans, the Ngakanes regularly hired members of labour-tenant households from nearby farms for particular purposes – reaping or butter-making – for which tasks they would be paid in kind.

In particular, Barney's sense of moral superiority (perhaps a product of hindsight) emerges in his reproof of other Africans for their lack of interest in 'farming for profit'; 'most of the Africans in those areas were interested in producing just for subsistence'. Partly because of the restraints of capital and labour, partly because of the servile relationships in which they were caught, perhaps (more important) because of different expectations of their place in the world, many Africans on the farms were content to render labour (or the labour of their children) to a white farmer in return for the right to live on white-owned land. They ran their livestock and ploughed their fields for their own benefit – but on a small scale, recalls Barney, 'because they spent most of the time working for the landlord'. They were not paid for their services: their labour was perceived as payment for their rights of tenancy.

It was usual for those contracted to render labour to work for the landlord three months per year, says Barney, and they would then be permitted to go to the industrial towns of the region to seek temporary unskilled employment, while their place on the farm was taken by another family member who would also work for three months. Thus, in sharp contrast to the sharecropping elite of the mid-Vaal region, like the Ngakanes, many such families were clearly already dependent on wages to supplement the modest product of the soil for their survival. But many labour tenants at the time did still have the means to farm independently; they could turn the soil using their own ploughs and oxen and tend and reap their crop. The time would soon come when fewer and fewer blacks on white farms were in a position to do so, and by the 1930s and 1940s farm labourers had been reduced by and large to proletarian status, albeit paid mainly in kind. It was the Ngakanes' special achievement that many of them were able to avoid that fate, as we shall see.

The landlord at Vlakplaas, Fanie Cronje, was clearly much enriched by the diligence and the productive resources of his tenants. He bought a Ford motor car, 'with the income from maize that he got from his tenants', says Barney, at a time when cars were a rarity. He lived in a large house at Vlakplaas, and as far as Barney could tell, did remarkably little with his life. He 'was a farmer, but hardly did any farming'. He owned cattle, sheep and horses, and also had camps of wild animals, mainly blesbok, which he sold periodically.

Cronje seems to have been a man ill-suited to prosper in an age of capital when the old Boer economy was being undermined and the old Boer landowners were hard-pressed to maintain their position in the face of mounting debt (contracted both because of the flood of speculative mortgage capital that had been infiltrating the countryside since the mineral discoveries, and because of the natural disasters of drought and disease and war devastation). For he was apparently an ill-educated man (Barney suspects he was semi-literate), and had no source of income beyond what he earned from the produce of Vlakplaas. He was thus an example of a transitory figure on the highveld – the white landholder who profited from the productive resources, the skills and the entrepreneurial instincts of the black sharecropping tenantry. 'I suppose he understood his economics better than most farmers did,' concludes Barney; 'and he was a wealthy man.'

Nevertheless, it was altogether predictable that Cronje's star would wane as the autonomous black commercial farmers declined in prosperity under the pressures of white popular resentment, white agricultural development and state intervention. Many years later when the Ngakanes were living on their own farm near Boons station in the western Transvaal, Barney's father met old Cronje on the road. Cronje had been sadly impoverished and was hawking grapes at the nearby diamond diggings. 'Look,' he told Marcus, 'if you people are willing to come back to me, I'm prepared to go and hire a farm.' 'That is typical of the economics of South Africa,' says Barney perceptively.

At Vlakplaas, Cronje was prepared to leave his tenants alone, visiting them only occasionally to enquire how they were getting on. Barney remembers him as easygoing, generous and approachable. He did not consider it to be demeaning to share a meal with Barney's parents in their own home. He apparently had a high regard for young Barney himself, and declared to his parents that the boy should be educated beyond the farm school. In many ways, men like Cronje were out of step with the mounting spirit of the times. His laissez-faire attitudes toward black economic enterprise were increasingly resented by whites, many of them of a younger generation, who understood that white dominance had to be asserted and fought for if the land was not to be taken over by foreign capital and black commercial farmers, and if the Boer rural economy was not to be expropriated.

Also on the farm (which was very extensive) were seven white bywoner families, who lived some distance away from the black tenant community, and with whom they had little contact. These Afrikaners, according to Barney, were not allowed by Cronje to employ black labour but had to perform the work in the fields themselves. They were poor, and all of them combined, asserts Barney, could not produce what each one of the black families produced every year. When pressed on the reason why the undercapitalised and less privileged whites on the land, the neighbouring bywoners, were so unsuccessful and were looked down upon with such contempt by the black sharecroppers, Barney responds that 'the reason was simply that it was their attitude towards labour. The Afrikaners, even the poorest of them, regard hard labour as a "Kaffir's" work. And the bywoners even wanted to have servants.' Farming techniques and the technology available to black and white were the same: 'it was all cattle traction and hard work,' says Barney. The black farmers accounted themselves superior both as trainers and handlers of ploughing spans and as workers in the fields, using as they did not only the labour of the entire family, but also networks of reciprocal labour based on kinship. 'The bywoners in the surrounding areas, they said, "We don't know when those *volke* go to bed. When we go to bed their fires are burning, when we get up in the morning their fires are burning."'

These contrasts between the declining class of white tenants and the prospering black tenants on the land were deeply resented by whites, particularly Afrikaners, who were increasingly being mobilised around the symbols of racial survival and racial threat. 'The surrounding white farmers did not understand why there should be prosperous black people. But the white farmers could do nothing because of this man Cronje,' says Barney. The greater success of black producers on the white-owned farms, and the fact that so many self-interested white landlords preferred black tenants over white (whatever their public prejudices and fears about white impoverishment might have been), spurred whites to action. This local crisis was a microcosm of developments throughout the arable highveld, which were to reach a climax within a few years of Union in 1910. Barney remembers these times vividly. He recalls:

'And it so happened one day, the first prime minister of South Africa, General Louis Botha, held a meeting on a farm belonging to a wealthy farmer, called Jan Muller, also in the Vereeniging district. All the farmers in the surrounding area attended. And my Dad and his brothers said, "Well, let's go and hear what the baas is discussing." So they went there and sat on the periphery of the meeting and listened. At the end of the meeting one farmer stood up and asked a question of General

Botha, whether it was right that there should be black people who were living a life of comparative ease, when there were *hundreds* of poor whites, bywoners. And the answer from General Botha was 'No'. Then the farmer, Cronje, got up and he asked, "Well, gentlemen, I have seven bywoners on the farm and I've seven black families, and I get from one of those black families what I cannot get from the seven bywoners together. Are you going to ask me to take food out of my mouth?" This was the way that he put it. And the next thing that happened there was that the farmers all said, *"Donner hom!"* ["Beat him up!"]. They were going to assault Fanie Cronje for saying that seven white farmers could not produce what one black farmer produced!

'And that was the beginning. Pressure was brought to bear upon Cronje after the meeting, and eventually he called my people together and said, "Now look, we're going to enter into a new contract. The terms of tenure should be changed." They said, "Now, what changes do you want to bring about?" He said, "Now look, you have many head of cattle, and I do not benefit from these cattle. Therefore, I'll give you two alternatives: either you register every calf that is bred so that in winter we come and share the calves or if you don't do that you sell all your cattle, and leave just about four cows for milk for the family needs and the trek oxen. Those are the new conditions of tenure which you have now got to accept." So my father then said to him, "Baas, you hadn't told us what you were calling us for; give us time to go and think." He said, "All right, you come again and tell me what you have thought." '

The community was in a quandary as to what was to be done. They were united in their determination not to submit to these depredations. But the Ngakanes were not alone. Throughout the highveld, countless individual ultimatums were being delivered as white landholders asserted their dominance over the production of their tenants. And new forms of resistance were being exploited too, as the Ngakanes soon discovered:

'Now, by a very strange coincidence, one of those things, you know, that just happen, a young men came from Johannesburg, and young people from Johannesburg in those days were not popular. They were regarded as rogues if they came from Johannesburg. They were *slim* [smart]. But this young man came and found the old man despondent and he said, "What is happening?" They told him. He said, "Why don't you buy your own farm?" My father replied, "Oh, but is a black man allowed to buy a farm?" He said, "Of course, yes!" He said, "There is a black attorney in Johannesburg. I'll take you to him, and through him you will be able to buy your own farm."

'Now there were two black attorneys in Johannesburg at the time, Mangena and Dr Pixley Seme. Seme is the man who started the African National Congress. So this young man from Johannesburg took my father to Seme, and eventually they were able to buy a farm near Boons, on the other side of Koster.'

A letter from Seme to Barney's uncle Paulus is still in the family's possession; in it the lawyer urged them to go and inspect the farm immediately and to keep the matter confidential, no doubt because of the anger his activities evoked amongst certain whites. Seme warned the Ngakanes in this letter that a bill then before parliament threatened to make black land purchase illegal, and haste was thus essential. The Ngakanes took this advice, and bought the farm (between Rustenburg and Ventersdorp) through the agent Seme. This transaction took place in

1913, shortly before the Natives Land Act, enacted later in the same year, prohibited all further land purchases by blacks outside areas earmarked for inclusion in the reserves. Seme was at this time actively engaged in helping blacks, threatened with dispossession and eviction in a period of rapid development and capital accumulation in white farming, to secure land free from the constraints imposed by increasingly intolerant white landlords. His energies were mainly channelled into the Native Farmers' Association of South Africa, which had bought a number of farms in the Wakkerstroom district of the eastern Transvaal. These farms, Driefontein, Daggakraal and Driepan, were sold off in ten-morgen plots to African smallholding farmers whose productive base was being undermined by the newly assertive white farmers, taking advantage of financial boom and government support to extend control over the rural economy in the aftermath of Union. In general, these were years of widespread land purchase by blacks seeking to use access to the land market as a weapon of resistance against the forces of dispossession.

Much land in Rustenburg and neighbouring districts was being bought up by blacks, sometimes by syndicates like the Ngakanes, more often by chiefs acting on behalf of their followers, who paid communally for the land. This resulted in widespread reactivation of (often historically tenuous, even fictitious) networks of kinship and ethnicity, and a resurgence in the authority and prestige of chiefly lineages that had in many cases long since ceased to perform any real political function. Much of this land was subsequently incorporated into the reserve areas (present-day Bophuthatswana); other black-owned farms were eventually sold or expropriated in one way or another, and only the occasional 'black spot' remains as a reminder to the ideologues of apartheid that the task of stripping black-controlled resources outside of the reserves is not yet complete.

The Ngakanes' new farm, Klipgat, comprised 1 019 morgen, and cost them 38 shillings per morgen. Fourteen families were involved in the purchase of Klipgat – the seven who lived at Vlakplaas plus seven others, all related by blood or marriage, all of the same generation. Some proved more reliable in the payment of instalments than others; but the financially stronger (like Barney's father) took up the slack on the understanding that the weaker ones paid back their debts as and when they could. There was 'complete unity amongst those old people', says Barney with admiration. A single inclusive title deed was issued; and each purchaser was given a subsidiary deed to an indivisible share of the farm. They were permitted to sell their shares, but purchasers had to join the syndicate and obey its regulations. The farm was cut up into grazing camps, and each family had its own arable fields of equal extent. Barney's eldest uncle Paulus was elected chairman of the community committee, and was succeeded by Barney's father, Marcus, in 1920. But Barney says that Marcus had always been the brains behind the scheme.

Barney's people did not leave Cronje's farm Vlakplaas until about 1920; their new farm was in an area which was less suitable for arable production. But they were able to send their surplus stock to Klipgat so as to prevent their landlord from appropriating it or forcing them to dispose of it. Cronje did not immediately know that his tenants were buying a farm. They told him that they had decided to dispose of their animals and asked for a permit to convey them to Johannesburg market. They sold some of the cattle in order to meet the deposit on Klipgat, and sent the rest to the new farm. When eventually Cronje got wind of what was afoot, his reaction, much to their surprise, was to marvel at their ingenuity and to share a sense of pride in their achievement, never imagining that his profitable tenants would ever leave him.

At about the same time as they were deciding to buy Klipgat, the Ngakanes on Vlakplaas were experiencing the effects of growing white hostility and intolerance on another front as well. Understandably, the Ngakanes' school, representing what seemed to whites to be a surging tide of black entrepreneurship and class mobility, evoked strong feelings of resentment. The hostility of local whites was brought to the boil by one incident which Barney remembers clearly. There was a white school not far away, and the two schools were both visited annually by a government school inspector. One year the inspector visited the black school first, and was highly impressed by what he saw. Barney recalls:

'The following morning he went to the white school and, in scolding the white teacher for his work, he said, "You should really have been the black teacher, and that black teacher, that 'Kaffir' teacher there, should have been the white man." That's what he said. And immediately thereafter, this man, Steyn was his name, he called a meeting of parents of the school children at which he gave a report. He said that he had been told that the "Kaffir" teacher was a better teacher than he. He was compared, contrasted, with this black teacher. So that was one reason why the school was closed.'

Pressure was brought to bear on this front too, and Cronje felt unable to resist his neighbours' disapproval. As black schools on white farms, like all else, survived on landlords' sufferance, the school was dismantled with little ceremony and no regard for the rights or sentiments of the black tenants. Many of the pupils, in Barney's words, 'never saw the inside of a school again'.

But the Ngakanes were more determined to pursue their aspirations than were their less privileged neighbours in the vicinity, and they had the productive base to sustain them in their resolve. Barney was sent to school in Evaton where his teacher, Mashabani, now lived. There he stayed with distant relatives, who mistreated him. But his father would hear nothing of young Barney's pleas to be allowed to return home; his education was all-important, despite the loss of his valuable labour in the family fields. Eventually Barney moved into his teacher's home, paying for his board by doing the cooking. He remembers:

'At Evaton we still had the same inspectors, and we didn't go beyond Standard four. Standard four was the highest. But the inspector got there and he found this little boy, and he said to the teacher, "Give him Standard five." The teacher had to draw up his own syllabus and take me into Standard five. I was alone. The following year he came and said, "Let him do Standard six." And, well, I went to Standard six.'

From there the bright young Barney went on to the Methodists' Kilnerton Training Institution east of Pretoria to train as a teacher. The boarding fees which his father paid amounted to £10 per year. Teaching, like the law or the church, was one of the callings to which young men of Barney's background and position might aspire. Learning and erudition were qualities that were highly valued in their social milieu. The capitalist values, creating and consuming wealth, were still alien, and did not sit well with the Christian idealism which permeated their world view. Meanwhile, Barney's sister was sent to an industrial school in Natal, together with four others from the community – Miriam and Johanna Ngakane, Elizabeth Lokoane and Ruth Digeso; and another sister became a nurse. There was no prejudice against the education of women in this family.

Kilnerton was an elite institution by the standards of the day. The Reverend Fred J. Bristoe was superintendent, and J. C. Johns was principal. Barney also remembers H. W. Puxley and D. E. Newman, Miss Bradshaw, Mrs Johns and Mrs Puxley on the staff. Many of these came from Westminster College in London. Like Lovedale in the Cape, a not dissimilar institution, reflecting the same values and ideals, Kilnerton prided itself on its commitment to the promotion of a black Christian elite in an age when such values must have seemed under increasing threat, even obsolete. But that did not mean that racial discrimination and a heavy-handed paternalism did not exist there, as Barney was to discover when he himself joined the staff. There were no black members on the staff of the training institution; blacks only taught at the neighbouring practical school. There, Ralph Nkosi, who subsequently became a Wesleyan minister, and a Mr Mphahlele taught the young Barney, and T. P. Mathabatha was principal of the practical school.

Barney stayed at Kilnerton for three years, still returning home to Vlakplaas every vacation to help with the family farming enterprise. During the winter harvest season, in particular, he spent his entire vacation in the fields, his father allowing him only one day's relaxation after his arrival home, and one day's rest before his return to the college. He was the youngest in his class, and recalls that at the end of his period there the inspector pronounced that he would have to stay on another year as he was too young to graduate. He was in his seventeenth year. Barney was one of the students chosen at random by the inspector to demonstrate his teaching skills and knowledge of the syllabus as a gauge of the accuracy of their teachers' assessments.

'So I was amongst those who were picked out by the same man who was determined to fail me. But I gave him a very pleasant surprise because . . . the same afternoon every teacher, white and black, came to congratulate me as the inspector had said, "I was determined to fail this boy, but his teaching was so good that I could not help but give him the highest marks." And then they thought I was too young to go and teach outside, and I was employed as a teacher on the college staff.'

Barney was on the teaching staff for nine months, but was not happy:

'When you are a young boy you feel you're going to control the whole world. I had hardly started teaching when I started quarrelling with the superintendent about the conditions of our meals and in the end I said, "Now listen, I've no confidence in the missionaries at all." I gave up teaching after just nine months. Then I went and stayed at home for three months trying to find another job. Then the Reverend W. Shilling wrote me a letter and said, "Now there's a little school near Piet Retief, and would you like to apply for it?" So I applied for the principalship of this little bush school. And I was there for a year. This was in 1920–1. And then again I quarrelled with my superintendent over a question of salaries. (*Laughs.*) When I left Piet Retief I came and taught in Sophiatown, then I went on transfer to Germiston, then got my first principalship in Springs. But after six months I was recalled to Kilnerton. So in

1926 I was back at the institution as principal of the practical school, next to the training college.'

Barney remembers the discriminatory conditions and salaries between the white and black staff. He also recalls that all notices were addressed to 'The Staff and the Native Teachers'. But it was also at this time, in the late 1920s, that the first blacks were appointed to the training college, the Reverend Mr Bolani, a Methodist minister, and Ezra Masiza. Barney also began running classes in academic subjects in the college.

The training institute at Kilnerton was a teachers' training college, and did not train its students for the matriculation examination; but at this time a secondary school was opened there, and Barney taught in this school too. Amongst his first students was Mary Malahlela, later Xhakane, who gained a B.Sc. degree and trained as a medical aid (requiring up to six years' formal training) at Fort Hare in the eastern Cape, before subsequently enrolling as a medical student at the University of the Witwatersrand in Johannesburg where she eventually qualified.

Barney married a fellow teacher at Kilnerton, Mabel Mzondeki from Johannesburg, in 1927.

What we see in this apparently tangential narrative is in fact a social transition, built on the commercialisation and transformation of the family economy. However, the family economy did not wither away with the turning of the generations as a result. It was fostered and sustained as the essential material foundation, the security and custodian of the extended family network. In this, too, the Ngakanes were entirely typical of their class. But they were less than typical insofar as they succeeded in becoming freehold landowners in their own right before this avenue to security on the land was closed off in

1913.

In the post-war boom years, the pressures of the pre-war years were again being felt by the sharecropping tenantry, whose contracts were now formally illegal under the terms of the Natives Land Act of 1913; and Barney's parents finally left Vlakplaas and settled at Klipgat in 1920. Barney did not stop contributing to the family economy, visiting the farm regularly until his father died in the mid-1960s. There the extended family continued to flourish as mixed farmers, although not on the same scale as in their days at Vlakplaas. But as landowners they had potential access to the sort of windfall profit which has so often been the concomitant of landownership on the South African highveld, and which has been the engine of so much capital accumulation amongst whites. In the 1920s diamonds were discovered on the neighbouring farm. Barney tells the story:

'Part of our farm also had diamonds, but it had to be proclaimed a public diggings. Now in terms of the law the owners of the farm, in this case my people, were entitled to 37 claims. They had to select 37 claims where they thought the most diamonds lay, before the place was proclaimed a diamond digging. They chose the 37 claims, then the place was proclaimed. Then the problem arose, the law did not allow a black man to handle a diamond. They had this diamond claim, but they were not allowed by the law to handle diamonds. And it meant they were going to employ a white man to sell the diamonds for them. So my Dad, he was not an unintelligent old man, he said, "Now this is a white man selling my diamonds to another white man. Now what's there to stop the two of them from dealing in such a way that both of them will benefit and I get nothing?" So in

1927 he asked his brothers, "Now look, instead of handling the diamonds at all let us sell our claims as they are, whether they find diamonds on them or not. Let's find somebody who is prepared to buy them – but he must give, not cash, he must buy another farm and pay all the costs and give the title deeds to that farm." They decided and the result was a second farm which we had at Lichtenburg. Some of the families are still there, but my father sold his right. So they got a second farm from the diamonds. Now actually, there, it was not the farm they sold, it was just what they called the precious stone rights.'

These rights were bought by a Mr Fine from Johannesburg, who also bought them the new farm near Lichtenburg further west – in his own name in order to bypass the provisions of the Land Act which prohibited black landownership. This story reveals quite a lot about the limits of social transformation amongst blacks. Obstructed in their wish to benefit directly from dealing in the minerals on their land, they were forced back again on ensuring access to land as the ultimate guarantor of their security – albeit in defiance of racial restrictions. Unable to enter the mainstream of capital accumulation in industrialising South Africa, their strategy was perforce limited to trying to consolidate what they had already achieved – a modest island of independent enterprise amidst the storm of dispossession and proletarianisation in which the great bulk of blacks on the land were caught up. The ties of community and kinship and the extended family economy, radically transformed as they had been by the dictates of commercialised production, survived because the racial order did not permit any really viable long-term alternative. Subsistence production remained a basic priority for them, in a world which must have seemed largely and increasingly hostile. It was left to whites to exploit the mineral riches of the soil and enjoy the fruits of embourgeoisement. Blacks were not allowed in that world.

It is not surprising then that Barney Ngakane, having from a young age been marked for better things than the life of a farmer and having acquired all the skills necessary for entry into the achieving classes, died not in suburban comfort, but in the desolate landscape of Bophuthatswana (though on his people's privately owned land), surrounded by the victims of the apartheid state. Much of Barney's adult life graphically reveals the limitations on black class mobility. His was a lifetime of service to the poor and downtrodden; but it was also a lifetime of submission to the class perceptions of white liberals. His role was determined and circumscribed by reformers whose own visions were shot through with the same paternalism and social distance which Barney had come to know at Kilnerton and which characterised relations on the 'European–Bantu Joint Councils' on which he sat from 1923, when teaching at Sophiatown.

His career in teaching ended in 1936 when he was employed by a committee under the chairmanship of J. L. Hardy, a Johannesburg lawyer, to run a reformatory for delinquent boys in Orlando. Here he also served as secretary to the township Advisory Board, appointed by the white municipal authorities. He then started the 'Orlando Lads' Hostel', along the lines of the Boys' Town concept. In 1943 he moved to East London to start a similar institution there. These interventions by white humanitarians were a response to the massive social dislocation of these years, as slum conditions proliferated on the outskirts of the rapidly industrialising cities. Not atypically amongst middle-class purveyors of social betterment, they saw the collectivisation of problem people in institutions as the answer to social and moral ills. On his return from East London Barney was appointed secretary of the Bantu Welfare Trust, which was involved in legal aid, funding schools in the townships and financing black medical students at Wits University. The Trust was also concerned to wean black trade unions away from Communist Party influence by shovelling funds and facilities in their direction, amongst a variety of other projects. During this time, right up through the 1950s, Barney was also heavily involved with the Institute of Race Relations as a field officer. In 1960 he opened a private advice office in Orlando to help people cope with the legal maze of the pass laws that constrained their lives ever more tightly.

In all these years Barney was closely involved with the network of white liberal reformers that had partially grown out of the Joint Councils established in the 1920s; and he always worked easily and without rancour (even after 1948) with the local white officials and occasionally the bureaucrats in Pretoria who in so many ways exercised arbitrary powers over the lives of blacks. But there was always a large degree of ambiguity in his attitudes toward those who presided over his fate. Even while he was playing a prominent role on the Joint Councils in the 1920s and 1930s, he was very critical of the subordinate role that blacks were usually expected to play and did not agree that white leadership was invariably a good thing. He also saw the danger that these bodies could pull the teeth of black political activity and draw black leadership away from political organisation and education.

In fact, Barney was also a firm supporter of the

African National Congress all his adult life. He played a prominent role in Congress politics from the mid-1930s on, eventually becoming Transvaal president in 1959, shortly before the movement was forced underground. The ANC was also strongly represented on the family farm Klipgat. Barney's parents were both members from early days; Marcus became provincial organiser for the western Transvaal, and Barney's mother was chairperson of the women's branch on the farm. And his son Pascal, who married ANC president Albert Luthuli's daughter and played a prominent role in the ANC underground in Natal in the early 1960s, spent time as a political prisoner on Robben Island before going into exile.

Barney's role in the organisation was always a conciliatory one; but in the 1950s he became wary of the dominating role of white leftists in the movement, developing a sympathy for Robert Sobukwe's Africanist wing of the party. But he did not support the Pan-Africanist Congress after it was formed, considering its formation an 'unnecessary dissipation of our forces'. His son Pascal, however, was to be unceremoniously expelled from the ANC because of his opposition to the Congress Alliance. Barney's belief in black self-sufficiency and self-reliance matured as he grew older. After he had gained a diploma in social work from Wits University, he helped to launch a Social Workers' Organisation in opposition to the existing body of black social workers that was firmly under white liberal control. When Barney was sent as ANC delegate to the founding meeting of the Liberal Party, he told those present that constitutional politics under white leadership had no role in the struggles of blacks, and clashed with Alan Paton over the issue.

Barney's political affiliations and activities often

caused tensions with his white patrons, the less sensitive of whom were unsympathetic toward black political initiatives that seemed to threaten their cosy mediating role. These linkages of patronage were in any case breaking down by the 1950s; and at the Institute of Race Relations in particular, Barney had to tread a narrow line in order to avoid offending whites who were often very threatened at the growing militancy of mainstream black politics. On the whole, throughout his life, he succeeded in negotiating with adroitness what Shula Marks calls the politics of the tightrope. But he could never quite escape the ambiguities of dependence. His social, cultural and geographical origins retained their hold on him. He might have been critical, even cynical, of the kind of world that the white liberals were trying to forge; but he was inextricably part of their world, and he remained so. He fought against some of the ideological assumptions of their brand of liberalism, the more so as he grew older, but he never resolved the contradictions which were inside him and which pervaded the society in which he and others like him lived.

But the apartheid state, less empathetic with these contradictions and crudely determined to force black political activities into the mould of its own pseudo-ethnic structures, caught up with Barney. He was banned for five years in 1963, just as the family's farm Klipgat was being expropriated as a 'black spot' and hence a blot on the idealised apartheid landscape. Barney's father Marcus, now a very old man and still living at Klipgat as chairman of the community of landowners there, was taken by H. B. Klopper of the Bantu Affairs Department whose job it was to organise removals, to see some land far in the northwestern Transvaal. This land was due to be incorporated in the

Tswana bantustan, according to the new policy of creating an ethnic 'nation' for each and every black South African, and a corresponding fictional 'homeland'. The landowners of Klipgat were given a farm, Uitkyk, in the northern Marico district, much less desirable and relatively much more remote from markets, but larger by perhaps 50 per cent than the land they had left behind. They were now to live in what was to become the nominally independent, fragmented state of Bophuthatswana, and no longer in South Africa as it was redefined. Barney considered that life in this dry, remote region might be more congenial than under virtual house arrest in Orlando, Soweto, and applied to the authorities for his banning order to be amended so that he could go and live there. This was granted. His father meanwhile had died, and Barney became the leader of the family community, or what was left of it.

The Ngakanes were not alone in being removed from their land. During the 1960s many thousands of Africans – few of whom were landowners like the Ngakanes – were being moved off land outside the reserves. As had happened at an earlier period when the bounds of freedom on the land were closing in rapidly – the years leading up to the passing of the 1913 Natives Land Act – Africans developed their own strategies of survival. The first line of defence lay in reformulating corporate identity. Once again, displaced people responded to their plight by laying claim to one or other ethnic identity, often historically fictitious, usually without much historical continuity, always designed to meet immediate needs. They had to develop new ways of legitimising claims to land and other resources within the Bantustans, not only according to the rules laid down by the ideologues of apartheid, but also according to social models which had a real purchase in their own historical experiences. Not for the first time in the history of the twentieth century, 'chiefs' emerged from the social woodwork, rural and urban, each with a greater or lesser claim to historical legitimacy, and followings sprang up where there had been none before. Even the Ngakanes, who had not recognised a chief for well over a century, were soon involved in the rediscovery of traditional forms. Barney tells the story thus:

'My Dad came to me and said, "Now look, we've got our little farm here, but the members of our tribe are all scattered around. Can we do something for them?" And I said, "Yes, Dad, let's do so if we can, by all means." Then we picked them out, picked out the old people and called them together in Orlando, and we told them what we were thinking. And they said to my father, "Well, go on." We went on, and I was secretary to the group. Now the old man was popular with the government officials. He had the respect, let me say, of the government officials. So whilst we were collecting money from the people and banking it, the government came to us and said, 'We are going to move you from Boons to here [to Uitkyk]." So my father then said to them, "Yes, good. We can't do anything, but we have taken money from people and told them that we are going to find them a farm. Can you find us a farm?" They said, "What people are those?" He says "The Bapogole, a branch of the Bafokeng." They said, "Yes, we read about them in the books, but where are they?" (*Laughs.*) My father replied, "Oh, they are all over the farms here." They said, "All right, we'll help you." Then my father died. So I carried on with the work and they [the officials] said to me, "Now look, you are going to settle on this portion which we are giving in exchange for your farm. As soon as the negotiations are through with the man from whom we are buying the other section, we are going to sell that to the tribe." So the negotiations went through, and then they came to me and I paid over the money to them.'

But not only was 'the tribe' reconstituted; a chief had to be found as well. Before Barney's father died, the Ngakanes had said to the Bapogole elders, 'Now look, we know that traditionally the chief should be such and such a family.' The family – the Mogagabes – was sought out in the townships of industrial South Africa and a chief was appointed. In all this, the Ngakanes and their collaborators – not least the apartheid bureaucrats of the Bantu Affairs Department – were guided by reference to Ellenberger's *History of the Basuto*. Thus Ellenberger, the early amateur ethnographer of the Basotho, whose research was deeply flawed and whose conclusions were dubious, was put to use in the legitimation of a new order which he no doubt could never have foreseen.

The wheel has turned full circle. Barney Ngakane's life encompassed, on the one hand, the early flowering of a new elite, ready to take its place in a new society of education, opportunity and enterprise; and, on the other hand, the eventual turning of that elite in upon itself, the destruction of social ideals and the reconstruction of archaic social forms. Barney Ngakane is dead, but he lives on in the community around the farm Uitkyk in Bophuthatswana. In his eighties he won a last, small, sweet victory from the bureaucrats created by the apartheid system. Despite opposition from both chief and magistrate, he managed to gain official recognition from the Bophuthatswana administration for a co-operative scheme designed to help the local families who lived on the 'tribal' land, and whose menfolk worked elsewhere as migrants, to earn a small income from the soil. But by the time he died, the co-operative, perhaps inevitably, had yielded no fruits. The victims of apartheid continue to subsist on remittances and little else.

However, the fraud of resettlement had become apparent in other ways as well. Within a couple of years of their move to Uitkyk, the bulk of the Ngakanes' stock had died in a disastrous drought. Moreover, by the time Barney died more than twenty years after the move, no title deeds had been issued to validate his and his relations' rights of ownership to the land that they had been given in return for their family farm near Boons station. This was a common experience amongst those Africans who had been landowners before the apartheid state had devised a way to deprive them of their land. Despite Barney's resort to Helen Suzman's skills, their struggle was for the most part a futile one.

Barney Ngakane maintained his dignity in old age; but only because he continued to resist the tyranny that had sought to strip him of his identity and his ideals and his history. When he died he was talking of writing his autobiography, so that future generations would understand where they had come from and never forget. His sons, who had learnt their politics at his knee and were supporters in exile of the nationalist movement, had become part of the 'communist threat' in the eyes of white conservatives around the world. This was perhaps an index of the victory of white supremacy in South Africa.

Winburg district, 1890s (photo: South African Library)

The Life Story of Petrus Pooe

Petrus Pooe (pronounced as in 'toy') was born on the farm Arcadia near Dover station in the northern Orange Free State in the year 1902. He remembers the small sharecropping community there as consisting of three households – that of his parents and his father's two brothers. His father's elder brother Ranchawe was also known as Mojakane – a Sesotho word derived from the English 'deacon', an indication of his standing in the community of Christian converts. Petrus's father was Abednoch, and the youngest of the three brothers at Arcadia was Lazarus. Apart from the three Pooe households, clustered together to form a small village, there were no other families in the neighbourhood. Their landlord at Arcadia was one Dannhauser. Petrus remembers that his father owned a lot of woolled sheep, whose wool was baled for sale at Arcadia station. They also had many head of cattle.

Like all the sharecroppers of the region they used double-furrow ploughs and harrows, but they broadcast their seed and did not use planters. They grew both maize and sorghum; the maize was purely a commercial crop, according to Petrus, as they used sorghum for subsistence, pounding it and making sour porridge, supplemented with milk from their cows. 'In fact, maize porridge as you know it today is of recent origin,' says Petrus, and was not made in the days of his childhood. It was only when he lived in Johannesburg that he became accustomed to eating maize meal. They sold their grain at Heilbron or Wolwehoek, transporting it by wagon; or locally at Dover station if the crop was small. That was 'real agricultural land' remembers Petrus, and farming 'was taken seriously' in those days. Each of the families ploughed its own fields, but the livestock was grazed communally. When asked how much they produced, Petrus responds that 'a hundred bags was nothing'. He says the ploughed lands were very extensive, and after a good harvest the grain was stacked high around their homes. 'Indeed, in the Orange Free State, the Boers had not become impertinent as they are today. They were quite co-operative in fact; often a black man would borrow a span of oxen, or else the white man would borrow a span of oxen from us for his own use.'

Typical of their class, the Pooes took education seriously, and were practising Christians of the Wesleyan persuasion, all of them contracting church marriages. There was a black school at Arcadia which they had built, and which doubled as a church, where several of the children from neighbouring farms as well as relations of the Pooes from further afield attended classes conducted by Naphtali Pooe, another of Petrus's uncles, and a man of some education. His successor as teacher at the school was one John Rampa. According to archival evidence, Rampa was also an organiser of an abortive union of black workers on the farms of the vicinity, formed to demand money wages for all labour service. Petrus himself apparently never went to the school at Arcadia, for reasons that are now obscure, and first attended school after they had left Arcadia in 1913.

As is the case with everybody who remembers life on the farms in the second decade of the century, the great crisis of the years leading up to the First World War is vividly recalled by Petrus Pooe. The upsurge of resentment amongst whites against independent black commercial farmers reached a crescendo in about 1913, and as was the case throughout the highveld, the Pooes found the boundaries of freedom closing in rapidly. As seems to have been very widely the case amongst sharecroppers at this time, their landlord demanded that his share of their crop be raised from a half to two-thirds, and that they reduce their excess cattle. This attempt by white landholders to extend control over productive resources was almost ubiquitous at this time, and had been building up for a number of years. The Pooes had already discovered that they shared a common interest with black tenant farmers like themselves over a very wide area; and, more than that, they had the potential for joint resistance, which was not to be available to later generations confronted with similar circumstances. Unlike the Ngakanes, whose resources were perhaps greater, the Pooes and others like them were forced to forge larger and more deliberately constructed networks of solidarity than were available to them in the immediate circle of their kin.

Already a few years before 1913, when the Natives Land Act not only sought to bring the weight of law to bear against the black sharecropping tenantry but also prohibited black land purchases, the Pooes were party to a large-scale communal scheme to buy land, involving many of the farm tenants in the region. The position of black commercial farmers on white-owned land was increasingly precarious, and it seemed clear to the far-sighted that the days of untrammelled opportunity on the farms were past. Petrus Pooe, who was very young at the time, recalls what happened:

'Our elders got together to consider the difficult period that lay ahead. The immediate option was that of tracking down our *morena* [chief] to brief him about the difficult times that were in view. They went up north to look for their chief [Mamogale, chief of the Bakoena at Bethanie near Brits]. . . . He listened to them carefully and promised to give full attention to their request. To put it in his own words he said, "I don't know, I will see. In any case I must talk it over with the Bakoena in council." The outcome of his consultations with the rest of the Bakoena resident at Bethanie was that Bethanie was too small. He then addressed the Orange Free State Bakoena group – our own elders including my father – and said to them, "Bethanie is too small even for us. For that reason I will not be able to accept you as residents here." He went further and asked them a question, "What do you think I should do?" Our elders replied and requested him to help them to find them a place elsewhere. Chief Mamogale wanted to know from them whether they had money to buy. They said that they did not have money but they had cattle. This was around 1910 or perhaps 1909. That is when all this took place. It was about at that time that this meeting took place.

'In 1911 Phiri-ea-Feta [a counsellor of Mamogale] came to the Orange Free State to inform our parents that there was a farm between Koster and Ventersdorp which would be a good buy. This report had to be formally brought to them as in fact they wanted to buy a farm close to Bethanie. But as that was not possible they had to look further afield. He however pointed out that the farm did not have good water resources. Our elders, being desperate to settle on a property of their own, assured Phiri-ea-Feta that they would solve the water problem as soon as they were there. Phiri-ea-Feta then asked them to start collecting money. The collection in fact took them three years. It had to take that long because their major source of money was their cattle, which were fetching a very low price at the time. A big ox would fetch only £5 or £6. In fact if your ox fetched £6 that was a very good sale. They disposed of lots of cattle that fetched this low price.'

The farm thus acquired, Swartrand, or Mogopa as it became known to the inhabitants, was bought in the name of Chief Mamogale, each family contributing something in the region of £75 toward the purchase price. There is now no way of knowing how many people contributed to the purchase of the farm, although Petrus says it was a great many, perhaps as many as a hundred. Chief Mamogale might well have had access to the advice of Pixley Seme, as had others seeking land at this time – like the Ngakanes.

But although the purchasers of Swartrand no doubt had good practical reasons for exploiting the chief's patronage, they were not all historically his subjects nor had they all recognised his authority over them. Indeed, their allegiance to Chief Mamogale was pragmatic and in some degree historically fictitious, although it was no less real for that. Many seem to have rationalised their submission to the patronage of the Bakoena chief by creating their own historical mythologies. Thus, the Pooes, who were in fact of a Phuting lineage, developed their own traditions of allegiance. Petrus tells us that his father's eldest brother Ranchawe informed him when the latter was an old man that Mamogale had always been their chief, even when they had lived in the Orange Free State. They too had originated in the Magaliesberg.

'He said that many of them were in the Orange Free State and remained there because of the wars of the nineteenth century. . . . Those who were in the Orange Free State, especially of Koena origin, would come together to discuss matters of common interest or to decide on sending a present to their chief Mamogale.'

This evidence might mean that a degree of ethnicity-building had already been in process amongst these individualised sharecropping households in the nineteenth century. Many of them had spent some time in Moshoeshoe's Lesotho in the decades immediately following the Difaqane, before gradually moving out onto the farms in the last few decades of the century to take advantage of the greater opportunities for commercial production available there. It is possible that new forms of identity had been emerging in Lesotho amongst people who had originated in the western Transvaal. But what is clear is that, in the circumstances of insecurity of the early twentieth century, a degree of *ex post facto* historical reconstruction to suit immediate needs was indulged in by a lot of people like the Pooes, living on the white-owned farms of the highveld, to justify their place in the new community being forged under the auspices of the Bakoena chief Mamogale.

Chief Mamogale exercised control over the Mogopa community through Chief More, his local representative. Petrus remembers that chiefly authority was quite strict in the early years of the settlement. 'They were still very strong and capable of enforcing their authority – quite often in a very coercive manner.' This authority was manifested most obviously in the way in which the physical settlement of the land was initially organised according to a hierarchy of seniority. Petrus Pooe tells us that all the people who contributed to the purchase of the farm were (or more properly became) 'Bakoena'; but there were distinct differences between the true Bakoena and those who originally belonged to other clan groupings (a category of identification which had long since ceased to have an important significance in the lives of most black people living on the highveld, especially since the slow dispersal of settlement from core areas which had been going on for centuries had been thoroughly disrupted by the Difaqane wars of the early nineteenth century). Petrus describes the 'real' Bakoena as the Bamogopa-oa-Dire, who settled at the top of the town – a typical Tswana-style urban settlement, it seems – which was situated on a hill slope. Then, he tells us, came Baramorola, Batlhapi, Batlase, Bampshe, other Baphuting groups, and so on. The Baphuting *kgoro* or ward to which the Pooes belonged included a number of other family groups such as the Banyakale, which he describes as the chiefly lineage of the Baphuting.

There was undoubtedly a creative process of clan reconstruction in progress, which bore relation to the need for staking claims to material resources rather than to any inherent tendency for people to cling to tradition. And the patterns that emerged did not necessarily reflect any historical authenticity; rather, historical forms were used to shape a wholly new reality, reflecting contemporary relationships of power and patronage amongst the Africans of the highveld at a time when the room for manoeuvre and initiative amongst individual families was diminishing. Indeed, there were individuals amongst those who contributed to the purchase of the farm who quite deliberately changed their names in order to join a particular clan group, from Mpshe to Molope in the case of Dinah Pooe's father.

Those who contributed to purchasing Mogopa were

probably very heterogeneous in terms of their economic bases and geographical origins, apart from the fact that they were all rurally based Sotho–Tswana-speakers. But the movers in the scheme, like the Pooes, seem to have had much in common. They were united partly by networks of kinship and intermarriage amongst what was by now a fairly distinctive socio-economic stratum of commercial black tenant farmers in the heartland of the arable highveld, and partly by networks of church affiliation, with all the cultural connotations that their brand of progressive Christianity entailed.

So it was that the Pooes (three brothers and their families), confronted with the ultimatum described earlier from their landlord at Arcadia, set off in about September 1913 for their new home, their three wagons pulled by spans of big red oxen. Petrus remembers that the Vaal River was in flood, and describes the difficulty experienced in crossing it above Lindequesdrif. 'I had never seen such drama in my life,' he says. He remembers his father feeling the depth of the water with the handle of his oxen whip, his brother Samuel leading the oxen into the water until it was swirling around his chin, the surging river dislodging bags of grain from the wagons. Other families, likewise the victims of ultimatums like the Pooes, were also trying to ford the river on their way into the Transvaal, where the white economy was less advanced and where there was more space for black farmers to re-establish themselves. At last they reached Swartrand and set about building their new home on the land allotted them. Petrus recalls:

'We started ploughing on arrival. It soon became clear to us that the place was indeed arid. There was drinking water neither for us nor for our livestock. My father looked for a suitable place where he could sink a well.

He finally found one and managed to find enough water for us. For the first time in my life I saw people using long ropes to bring water to the surface. We built a few containers for our cattle and went on like that for some time. Now cattle, horses and people drank from a single well after a lengthy process of bringing the water to the surface. After a few years we bought a manual pump that had a wheel and a handle.'

The ploughing lands at Mogopa, on the southern part of the farm, were relatively small, certainly in comparison with what they had been used to in the Orange Free State. About six acres was the size of the average household's fields. Thirty or forty bags of grain were all that Petrus's family could hope to produce under the circumstances. The infertility of the soil and the aridity of the area made them dependent on the hardier grain sorghum, especially the strain Petrus remembers as *manjagane* (which he says is no longer available), rather than the more vulnerable maize. However, sorghum required far more attention during the growing season than did other crops like maize. 'Grain sorghum is very difficult to grow,' says Petrus. 'Apart from the handling, you have to look after the field, especially from the time the plants start bearing. One has to spend long hours in the fields driving away the birds, and at times, the locusts too. A sorghum farmer has to trim his fields, put up scarecrows, and be there in person every morning and every evening to drive the birds away. That in itself is a lot of work that should not be taken lightly.'

Furthermore, access to grazing land was inevitably far more restricted at Mogopa than had been the case on the farms they had left behind; and overgrazing had its impact quite quickly on the livestock of those who had settled there, especially as many who were not settled on the farm sent livestock there in the care of relations or friends rather than dispose of it at the behest of their landlords. Petrus's family lost most of their sheep in little time, killed off by disease. Not only was there intense competition for the best grazing areas, but the cattle again and again strayed into the arable fields to feed on the growing grain. 'In fact the pastures were very small and on the whole the farm was not adequate for the people and the stock on it,' says Petrus.

Life at Mogopa was altogether more precarious than on the farms of the northern Orange Free State. Not only was water scarce; the disease that Petrus calls *lebete* struck some time after the First World War with devastating results, and many of the inhabitants lost virtually their entire herds. The disease is endemic to the area and continued to plague the community. By contrast, says Petrus, 'the Orange Free State countryside had no strange animal diseases that posed such permanent threats as did the diseases here.' In 1918 the notorious influenza epidemic struck – the *drie dag* ('three days' disease'), so named as it took three days to kill its victims. The graveyard at Mogopa is filled with those who were killed by it. Petrus thinks that the majority of those who had come from the Orange Free State died as a result of the affliction, including a number of his own extended family.

Many of the purchasers did not settle at Mogopa, maintaining their position on the farms on which they had previously lived, or on other white-owned farms, but retaining their right to move to Mogopa when their position deteriorated. One such was Petrus's uncle Naphtali Pooe, who never moved there, but was buried there on his death many years later. In due time, Mogopa became too overcrowded to provide a viable alternative to those with livestock who were faced with dispossession on the farms elsewhere. Many newcomers arrived, relatives, tenants, squatters, as life on white-owned land became more precarious, and many of the original families moved off or became increasingly dependent on labour migrancy for their survival. More land was bought from a white farmer on the eastern side. This greatly extended the settlement, but the process of proletarianisation had proceeded too far to be reversed, and as time passed it was more and more impossible for all but the most privileged to work the land.

The Pooes' farming enterprise inevitably went into a sharp decline, and after the community and their livestock resources had been decimated by disease, the younger members of the larger family moved off in search of wage employment. Petrus first worked for white farmers in the vicinity of Mogopa as an adolescent, and then was employed in the kitchen of a white boys' boarding school in Ventersdorp. After a spell in Potchef-stroom, he finally made his way to Johannesburg. In the 1920s he worked for a butcher, delivering meat on a push bicycle, amongst other jobs, always sending money home to his parents, under whose authority he still considered himself to be. Occasionally he returned to Mogopa to help the more privileged families as well as neighbouring whites in ploughing or harvesting, for which he was paid in kind. But his own family was not able to sustain its own farming activities, despite the occasional purchase of livestock.

It was during this period that Petrus remembers one day seeing sixteen black men inspanned before a laden wagon on the road near Potchefstroom, a vision which he recalls with a sense of amazement to this day, and which symbolises for him the extreme cruelty of whites.

'They were a full span of sixteen men, inspanned and pulling a wagon. I stood and stared as I could not believe my eyes. At first I was not even persuaded that they were people. As they had short trousers on they looked like ostriches. I then thought that it was a Boer using ostriches as draught animals. I drew nearer. But luckily, before I got close, I met an elderly man who saw that I was puzzled by what I saw. He anxiously shouted and beckoned to me. I could hear from his shouting that he had something urgent to tell me. He told me to disappear at once as I would be shot by the Boer who had inspanned people like animals. I obeyed him and went off in the opposite direction. He told me that the men that I had seen were convict labourers being used on the farms. "Those people are prisoners and the man with the gun and the whip is very cruel. Never stare at him like that." I continued on my way still puzzled that human beings could be used like animals to pull a wagon. Son! I have never ceased to wonder whether what I had seen were real men, pulling a wagon. To this very day I am still shocked.'

Petrus, a man without strong political feelings, says that when he thinks of the indignities generations of Africans have had to endure, 'I have every reason to support our grandchildren for refusing to submit to any form of oppression.'

In 1932 Petrus married at Mogopa, and took his bride, a girl of the Makheledisa family, to Johannesburg. 'We left this place [Mogopa]. I had not built a house we could move into or made other arrangements. The house that you see I built many years later. Subsequently I came back from time to time and eventually decided to build here even though I lived in Johannesburg.'

So even though he maintained his ties of family and

identity with Mogopa, which remained his home base to which he would eventually return on retirement, he was now a fully urbanised Johannesburger. For something like twenty-two years he worked at the fresh produce market in Newtown. He and his family lived as tenants of one Kgengwe in Bertha Street, Sophiatown, the freehold township that was finally bulldozed by the government in the 1950s. Their children were born there. The one remaining son was in the early 1980s a factory worker in Maraisburg, and his wife worked for a white household as a maid.

Petrus Pooe and his children had never succeeded in acquiring sufficient education to be anything other than unskilled wage employees in town. When asked why he did not proceed with his education, Petrus responds: 'In fact in those days schools were not run the way they are nowadays. The major job for boys was looking after cattle. A boy did not have the full week to himself for schooling. We each went to school in turn. That is why we never became really educated.'

Apart from individual commitment and priorities, there was, not atypically, a direct relationship between the labour requirements of the household and the opportunities for education. Schooling was limited by the immediate needs for family labour. Petrus remembers the school at Mogopa which was built under the auspices of the chief. Job Mpshe and one Ramonkgoro were the first teachers; later came a Pedi named Ramushu and one Motuba. Petrus thinks he started attending school in 1916, when he was already a teenager, and when the family farming enterprise was already in decline. Not surprisingly, he did not proceed very far, as his family was becoming more and more dependent on wage income for their survival, and he had

to go out and earn money. Unlike their life in the Orange
Free State, at Mogopa 'it was not possible to stay at
home, plough the soil and sell the harvest in order to buy
what you needed'. Petrus cannot remember any young
men of his generation who stayed at Mogopa as farmers.
'Many of us left for Johannesburg. Many got married
there; many worked and died there. Some did come back
home, others did not. Some even left Johannesburg for
other places.'

Petrus gives other reasons as well for his resort to
urban wage employment. 'We wanted to be gentlemen,'
he says. 'We wanted to wash, to be clean and well
dressed.' In his memory the lure of fashion was
powerful. 'There was a make of trousers called "ragtime" which were in vogue at the time. Our friends would
come back from Johannesburg with these trousers on.
We would then think to ourselves that we could be like
them if we too went to Johannesburg. We looked down
on young men who walked bare-footed and had cracked
feet covered with red soil all the time.'

Petrus particularly remembers a male-voice choir led
by a young man named Rampulana which occasionally
visited Mogopa to perform. 'They would come on a
Friday well-dressed, clean and truly well-groomed to the
amusement of all the local populace. It was after such
occasions that most of us would take to rethinking our
positions. No sooner would they be gone than we would
decide to try our luck on the Rand as well.'

The inferior status accorded to the life of the farmer,
working with his hands in the soil, was apparent to all
those who valued education as a key to progress; but the
supposed superior attractions of urban living had not
always been evident to people like the Pooes. Many of
the more successful black sharecropping farmers in

earlier days, the Ngakanes for example, seem to have looked down on those who lived in urban locations: after all, there were no opportunities for accumulation available in the towns comparable to those available on the land. But when such opportunities for independent accumulation on the land had disappeared, as they did sooner or later for almost all blacks, what was left for the unattached young man was urban employment. In effect, the young Petrus's hankering after urban fashion as personified by Rampulana's travelling singers, represented the dying of older ideals held by his parents' generation. Investment in upward class mobility on the basis of rural enterprise gave way to investment in ragtime trousers.

Born in the same year as Barney Ngakane, with a similar family background, in a social milieu that prized progress and improvement through education above all else, Petrus failed to make the essential initial breakthrough into the new elite that only schooling could bring. Once that opportunity had been lost, it was in all probability lost for good. In the slumyards and locations of the Witwatersrand, the resources for upward mobility were virtually impossible to come by.

When he eventually went on pension, Petrus Pooe returned to Mogopa where he had meanwhile built a house. The insecurities of life in the urban areas of South Africa placed a premium on continued ties to rural communities, and in this too Petrus was typical. He had retained his rights there, not only as a home base to which he could retire and as a community on whose succour he could rely in case of need, but also as a sanctuary to which his descendants could resort. Thus his children sent their own children to Mogopa to be brought up by their grandparents, in the absence of a home in the urban areas where they had lived and worked all their lives, and in the absence of any chance of securing one. Those who had bought rights at Mogopa in the second decade of the century in the hope of preserving the rural household economy, had failed in their primary strategy. But in succumbing to the forces of proletarianisation, they had succeeded in securing a rural base, beyond the reaches of the white authorities (or so they thought), where they could build their own homes and rely on an extended system of mutual support from the community of kinsfolk (real or imagined), and where they could retire. Mogopa had in fact become a classic labour reserve, inhabited for the most part by the families of migrants, by old people and children, by the unemployed or underemployed, and by daily or weekly employees on the farms and in the towns of the immediate vicinity.

Although the opportunities for profitable farming at Mogopa were limited and short-lived, nevertheless many of the old families (like the Pooes) retained rights to arable land which they had no hope of working in the absence of productive resources, particularly plough oxen, and in the absence of male labour. But the social processes initiated by the apartheid state have never been without their ambiguities. The impoverishment of the many has always brought opportunities for the few. A new type of entrepreneur has arisen in the interaction between the urban nexus and the rural reserve. Petrus Pooe describes the situation at Mogopa as it developed in recent decades:

'There are many lands. People are not here to plough them. The only group of people who are capable of producing enough from the fields are those who have tractors. In fact the tractor owners are the people who are making money here. If they plough for you, out of ten bags you, the owner of the land, get one bag. Some of them do get sympathetic with their clients. If you are lucky you might get as many as two bags. Beyond that you get nothing. What I am saying is that we have the land, but we are incapable of putting it to use. Only those with tractors can. In order to survive as a farmer you must have a tractor. Apart from its being expensive you also have to hire a driver if you buy one.'

Thus some old patterns recur in new guise. Sharecropping relationships, once so central an element in the rural economy of the arable highveld region, have been resurrected; but now it is impoverished blacks who contribute the land, and much more prosperous tractor owners – who might be black or white – who do the farming. Innumerable small, powerless landholders confront an entrepreneur without whose resources of capital and labour and access to markets the land would be useless. The grossly unequal balance of power between the contracting parties is reflected in the share of the crop – 90 per cent – which the entrepreneur is able to claim for himself. The experiences of the Mogopa community in this regard can be replicated many times in the black rural areas of contemporary southern Africa, and are typical of the economics of labour reserves. One change that has taken place is that sorghum, the hardier but more labour-intensive crop, is no longer grown, as there is not enough labour available to take care of it during the growing season. 'In earlier times we used to be helped by the children,' says Petrus. 'Today that is no longer possible. The children today are nurses and teachers and therefore not available for work in the fields. Things have changed. Well, I agree with them. Their elders have gone through difficult times.'

There is another pattern that re-emerges here: the relationship between non-agricultural income and rural enterprise. As we have seen, from the earliest days of black commercial farming on the highveld, access to higher off-farm income (usually a function of education) implied a greater productive capacity on the land. Similarly, the contemporary black rural entrepreneur of the sort who buys tractors and works the land of migrant families unable to work the land themselves, is often also the owner of trading licences and small businesses in Soweto or elsewhere, with privileged access in some instances to the patronage of the local state in town and countryside. The apartheid system has spawned its black beneficiaries as well as its black victims.

But Mogopa was deemed to be a 'black spot', isolated from the nearest part of Bophuthatswana by miles of white-owned farmland, and it had thus to be expropriated and its inhabitants resettled elsewhere in order not to disrupt the neat racial order the apartheid regime planned in the countryside. The struggle for Mogopa elicited considerable international media interest. Perhaps no single forced removal of African people did more to focus worldwide attention on the ghastly realities of life under apartheid than the destruction of Mogopa. The state exploited conflicts within the chiefly family at Mogopa, the Mores, by extending recognition and promises of favoured access to resources at the proposed new site to its own protégé, Jacob More, an ex-policeman. Having secured the services of a collaborator whom they recognised as the representative of the community, the state officials proceeded to soften up the community by destroying the school and church buildings, and by removing the engines of the water pumps on which the inhabitants relied for domestic water supplies. Despite declarations, designed to placate the outside world, now thoroughly aroused by the long and much publicised struggle of the people of Mogopa, that forced removals were not official policy, police encircled the settlement in the early hours of 14 February 1984. The inhabitants were forcibly loaded onto trucks with what belongings they could carry with them, and were transported to their new home Pachsdraai in Bophuthatswana, not far from Barney Ngakane's home at Uitkyk.

But just as the state had turned to the chiefly family to legitimate the destruction of the community, so many members of the community rediscovered, as had their elders three-quarters of a century before, the utility of ancestral identity and chiefly patronage in the struggle for communal resources. Throughout the struggle to prevent expropriation the inhabitants were presented in the sympathetic media as the 'Bakoena tribe' and the land as 'tribal' land. The image of an undifferentiated, harmonious community being ruled in traditional fashion by 'tribal elders' was presented to the outside world.

Moreover, many of the families that were removed from Mogopa, perhaps most, ended up, not at the resettlement camp of Pachsdraai, but at Bethanie, where the Bakoena chiefly lineage, descendants of Mamogalc under whose auspices the original settlement at Mogopa had been created, still lived – now with the added patronage that came with recognised status within the Republic of Bophuthatswana. For reasons that were not dissimilar to those which motivated their forebears in about 1910, many preferred to attach themselves to a recognised chief with patronage to dispense and access to the patronage of the state. The building or rebuilding of ethnic ties and chiefly allegiance remains the response of the defenceless to dispossession. As for Petrus Pooe, he was in his eighties when the government trucks came. What became of him we never discovered. His life encompassed the birth and the death of the community known as Mogopa.

PART TWO

Social Transformations on the Highveld

The handful of life stories presented here vividly reveal many aspects of the rise and consolidation of the racial order from the perspective of the victims of that process. What strikes one is the richness and variety of these experiences, and the range of information contained in the oral record pertaining to social and economic life. When set in the larger historical context, the reminiscences of obscure individuals begin to reshape our understanding of major forces of social change. Stories such as these are not simply embellishments of the historical record, nor are they merely alternative subjective perspectives on the objectively established past. Large questions are raised here for our consideration; large areas of human history are revealed to view for the first time; established interpretations and images of the past are revealed as inadequate or misleading. Human history is an organic totality, and new perspectives and fields of enquiry cannot be merely tacked on to old, without calling into question much of the conventional wisdom that has shaped previous overviews of the past.

All sorts of hidden dimensions of the past are revealed in the life histories of obscure people. We have seen in these pages some very large-scale processes of social change at work in the small-scale context of individual and family experiences. From iron-age cultivators and herders organised in lineages and living mostly in small autonomous communities, the Sotho–Tswana people of South Africa's interior regions have in a century and a half become fully integrated into a racially structured industrial economy, albeit for the most part as a dominated, insecure, propertyless underclass. By examining in close detail some of the human dimensions of this history we begin to see some of the dynamics of class formation at work. Issues of culture, identity and consciousness come to the fore. The importance of individual initiative and class aspirations becomes apparent, even within the tight and overweening constraints of the developing racial order. Blacks were never just victims (although they were certainly that); they were also the makers of their own world in myriad ways. Every life story makes this apparent.

But, more than that, the oral testimony reveals quite clearly that blacks have not travelled a steady upward continuum from primitive to more civilised life, as conservative whites and the official mythology still so fondly imagine. Nor indeed does the image of exclusion, of denied opportunities, common in more liberal interpretations of the past, encompass the experiences revealed in the oral record. The concept of exclusion does not encompass the processes of dispossession, of stripping of resources, of (to be blunt) the *destruction* of emergent classes, that have been the lot again and again of blacks in South Africa. Blacks participated fully in the accumulative dynamic in early industrial South Africa. The degree of class mobility amongst black commercial farming households in the late nineteenth and early twentieth centuries has never been fully understood or appreciated by blacks or whites. Nor have the full dimensions of the experience of dispossession ever really been reflected in the conventional views of the past. When the experiences of the victims of white class power are brought centre-stage, they tend to reformulate our understanding of the larger forces at work in shaping contemporary South Africa.[1]

The black farming elite on the highveld was typically made up of people whose sense of identity and of political community had been tenuous and flexible over a period of two or three generations as a result of the upheavals of the early decades of the nineteenth century. They were exemplary of an important stratum of black South Africans who for several generations (in fact as far back as the Difaqane) have been formed in the nexus of the mission station, wage employment, farm tenancy, school, town and township, and in the process acquired a culture and a set of aspirations and assumptions about the world and their place in it that were radically different from those of their ancestors.[2] Many of these people on the highveld had at some stage in the course of the nineteenth century sought refuge within powerful reconstruction chiefdoms such as that of Moshoeshoe, but took the opportunity sooner or later to recolonise the wide plains north and south of the Vaal River where land was available and the opportunities for individual accumulation greater, albeit under the patronage of white landlords.

The seminal development in the latter decades of the nineteenth century was, of course, the mineral discoveries and the rapid urban growth which they set in train. The mineral revolution initiated a radical transformation of the rural hinterland, which took several decades to work its way through, and which was eventually to re-order societies throughout the subcontinent.[3] For those living on the arable highveld, the rise of local markets for grain crops provided possibilities for commercialisation and capital accumulation that had not existed before. Black farmers responded by taking advantage of opportunities to enter new relationships with white landowners (amongst whom corporate interests and absentee speculators were increasingly important), enabling them to farm profitably. Sharecropping arrangements (farming on the halves) took on a new meaning in this new era of large-scale market production, and became a widespread and in some districts predominant economic relationship. It was in large degree on the basis of sharecropping relationships that urban markets were initially fed, and it was partly on the basis of black sharecropping enterprise that many white landholders were able to benefit from supplying such markets.[4]

On the farms the extended multi-generational homestead was eroded from within by the forces of economic change just as it was being eroded from without. As land was subdivided and grazing became scarcer – a process well under way by the second decade of this century – so families split up and the authority of patriarchs over entire village communities disintegrated. New sources of accumulation that were available to young adults, and their growing reluctance to tolerate the control of seniors over resources, labour and income, caused fission and atomisation, just as the large concentrations of livestock of extended family communities were becoming more and more unwelcome to the white landholders. From the start, new settlement patterns and social forms were coming into being. But, simultaneously, blacks were discovering that white landlords were likely to place increasingly stringent obstacles in the way of extended black accumulation, as landed resources became scarcer and more valuable. The ambiguity of the sharecroppers' position was that the more successful they were (to their own as well as their landlords' benefit), the more vulnerable to dispossession they were likely to become. The seeds of their destruction were present from the start.

The typical sharecropping household in the early twentieth century was more nearly a nuclear household, though retaining close ties of kinship which continued to be the guarantor of its success and security. Sharecropping communities tended to be related by blood or marriage, although each household typically operated as an atomised, individual productive unit. The sharecroppers had access to a large family network for labour requirements, and could tap communal resources to survive the devastating effects of drought or animal disease or war. Alongside new social forms, new technology was adopted. Double-furrow ploughs, planters and harrows became commonplace. Threshing was increasingly performed by itinerant steam-thresher operators. The possession of ox-drawn transport wagons became indispensable to successful family farming.[5]

The black agrarian elite emerged and was sustained in the interaction between the field and the classroom. Rural accumulation laid the material foundation for the rise of incipient elites that was occurring throughout black South Africa; but in an oddly circular way, class mobility sustained the viability of rural production and fed into the processes of rural accumulation. Higher educational attainments meant access to higher wage and other off-farm income, and this in turn meant a greater potential for rural accumulation. Commitment to education was closely related to a commitment to a particular brand of improving Christianity. It was their Christian respectability and idealism that marked them out most obviously as an emergent elite. Christianity for them was a path to cultural inclusion and self-improvement.

Of course, this process of stratification was not universal, and quite possibly the rise of accumulating elites of the sort described here was more advanced in certain regions – such as the mid-Vaal districts in the heart of the arable highveld – than in others. But the historical significance of the processes at work, the rise of black commercial farming and the new cultural forces that were being built on the basis of rural enterprise, should not be underestimated. In many ways the black farmers were in the forefront of the new social classes emerging out of the cauldron of South Africa's industrial revolution. As these processes of accumulation amongst sharecroppers developed, so it became more and more difficult for outsiders to break into the ranks of commercial farmers. The ethics of neighbourliness eroded; and one finds clear signs of class consciousness in some informants' memories of early life. It was quite clear to them who were the 'insiders' – defined by kinship (real or fictive), schooling, church membership – and who were the 'outsiders', those caught in far more servile relationships, with very different attitudes toward family enterprise and self-improvement.

The black oral record also throws light on the processes of accumulation and social change amongst whites on the land. Invaluable insights can be gleaned on the origins, the development, and the dynamics of the white capitalist farming economy. What is strikingly apparent is the extent of white dependence on black productive effort in the early decades of the industrial era. It is evident that many whites on the land became very reliant on black tenants for their survival as landowners, in the face of creeping indebtedness and intensifying pressures on their self-sufficiency. By the twentieth century the Afrikaner landowners had been sucked in myriad ways into relationships of credit and indebtedness; and they did not have the range of economic options (trade, transport, hunting, transhumant grazing) that their grandfathers had enjoyed. Specialisation and intensive production were the prerequisites for survival, and these required a level of education and know-how that many Boers lacked. It would probably be true to say that black resources, skills and enterprise kept a whole generation of Afrikaners afloat on the land.

Of course, this is not to deny that white capitalist farming was also developing rapidly at the same time. New settlers of British and colonial origin were continually arriving in the arable interior regions of South Africa, bringing capital and expertise with them, particularly at times of financial boom when mortgage capital and credit were readily available, such as in the early 1890s, immediately after the Anglo–Boer War, and in the years after Union in 1910. There were wealthy landowners (English- and Afrikaans-speaking), who had made their money outside of the farming sector, in speculation, in the professions, in industry, in trade and transport, and invested in capitalist farming enterprises. The rise of black farming in the early years of the industrial revolution was accompanied by the capitalisation of white farming.

But there was no inevitability about the eventual victory of white capitalist farming, based on the employment of black labour, over the peasant sector – natural though this may seem from the vantage point of the present. In many respects the black tenantry had the competitive edge over the white farmers. Their costs were lower, as were their risks. Their relatively greater self-sufficiency and the use of family labour made them more resilient than whites, whose hold on land in many cases became more and more precarious. The communality and reciprocity that characterised the black economy protected them in some degree from the destruction of resources that is recurrent in agriculture – given the uncertainties of climate and markets. Moreover, the basic technology that was available to black and white alike was entirely compatible with family farming. In fact, it took massive state intervention – in the provision of schooling, of capital and credit, of expertise and technical services, and of marketing facilities – to lessen and eventually displace the dependence of so many white landholders on black surpluses, and to promote new generations of whites to the status of capitalist farmers, no matter how precariously many of them laid claim to that status.

The drive to establish a fully capitalist, white-controlled agriculture was based on a powerful social ideal, which cannot be reduced to narrowly economic considerations. The assertion of class power over blacks on the land was built on compelling racial imperatives. At the level of public rhetoric, the black farmers were widely regarded as an intolerable menace and threat to the dominance of the white race. White supremacy could not be taken for granted; it had to be constantly asserted and fought for, not only on the level of public policy, but in all areas of social and economic interaction between black and white. These ideas were tirelessly propagated by the emergent populist intelligentsia, many of whom, although not all, framed their concerns in terms of Afrikaner ethnic symbolism.

The sensitivity of whites was greatly sharpened by populist agitation and intimidation, particularly in periods of rapid change and development, such as marked the years after Union, and again in the mid-1920s. A new South Africa was being born, in rural as much as in urban areas, and the structures of dominance and control had by no means been settled. It was feared by the purveyors of public opinion, especially in the emergent Afrikaner nationalist movement in the early decades of the century, that whites on the land, many only barely surviving, were severely threatened by the combination of big capital and low-cost black family farming, which together seemed to be inexorably ousting them from any meaningful foothold in the industrialising economy. These fears were crystallised out particularly in the intense moral anxiety aroused by the so-called 'poor white problem' and the presumed 'degeneration of the race' that was the inevitable consequence of white impoverishment.

The rural blacks of the nineteenth-century highveld – cultivators and herders integrated in greater or lesser degree in market relationships, involved in arrangements of partnership or clientage with white landlords, some in more servile positions than others, some more independent and prosperous than others – were reduced uniformly to a working class during the course of the first half of the twentieth century. The intervention of the state in re-defining relationships by statute was a crucial element in this process, but was not the primary driving force. Governments can rarely engineer social change of this kind simply by passing laws. No state has that kind of power. It was the recurrent mobilisation of racial energies at a local level in an infinity of small ways in pursuit of a powerful social ideal that wrought the

139

transformation of the countryside.

We can see the process at work in the lives of black informants. Surges of dispossession were experienced at certain times of rapid economic development and heightened sensitisation amongst whites to the big issues of black competition and racial threat. In the memories of many black people from the heartland of the arable highveld, the years immediately preceding 1914, for example, have a special significance. The year 1913 saw the passage of the Natives Land Act, the law that on a number of levels laid down the foundations of the whole policy of segregation/apartheid as it was to evolve in subsequent decades. The Act also formally prohibited sharecropping and all other forms of rent payment by black tenants other than labour service; and it prohibited the purchase of land by blacks outside the reserves in order to stop them from resorting to the land market as a means of resisting dispossession (a development that is vividly revealed in some of the stories told in this book). The state thus early on nailed its colours to the mast of white supremacy in the countryside.

But it was not directly the Land Act that caused the traumatic experiences of dispossession and displacement amongst black farm families at the time. Legislative intervention was a reflection of heightened public awareness, alarm and debate over these issues amongst whites; but it did not of itself initiate the rural upheaval. Informants remember that during these years, they were obliged to sell off their 'excess' livestock, to render increased labour to white landlords, hand over a larger proportion of their crops in rent, and generally to place themselves and their productive resources more closely under white control. White landlords were flexing their muscles and asserting their dominance at the point of production. In 1913, these forces culminated in a mass dispersal of resistant and 'unproductive' blacks off the land, the first 'forced removal' on a large scale from the white-owned farms of the highveld, and as such the forerunner of much human tragedy that continues to this day.[6]

The provisions of the Land Act were not in fact implemented by the state. Sharecropping did not disappear, as the law dictated. When the dust settled, productive patterns had not been dramatically transformed all at once. The fact is that the forces of dispossession were not initiated or implemented by the state, but by hundreds of white landholders, responding to the call to blood and race. White domination had effectively been asserted. But white agriculture was not yet as capitalised as it was to become; white dependence on black resources and black enterprise had not yet been displaced. The transition to a fully capitalist, racially exclusive agriculture, was to be long drawn-out and never clear-cut. This story was to be repeated, perhaps in less dramatic fashion, in later periods of rapid development in white agriculture, perhaps with different regional foci, as and when the state-sponsored transfer of capital into white farming created the opportunities and the incentive for the further assertion of white capitalist domination over blacks on the land.[7]

The destruction of the black rural economy had profound cultural implications for the rising black elite on the land. Religion was a crucial aspect of this. Once white hostility had begun to close off avenues of accumulation and the educated began to feel the full weight of racial supremacy, Christianity gradually changed its social function and its appeal. It became a means of cultural resistance and self-assertion. The unquestioning commitment to white churches and education as a means of social mobility espoused by many of the early commercial farming families gave way, more or less rapidly, to religious self-sufficiency, and the mainline establishment churches lost much of their appeal. The Christianity of inclusion, of optimism, of improvement, faded, and was replaced by a Christianity that spoke more directly to the experience of racial exclusion and domination. A religion of universalism gave way to a religion of resistance and cultural self-reliance. Simultaneously, perhaps more gradually, mission education lost much of its appeal; and by the time the state finally destroyed the earlier idealism by appropriating black education directly as a tool of the apartheid order, a whole new disillusioned generation had already learned the hard way that the individualism preached by the mission teachers was not the liberating force their parents had imagined.

Similar forces to those operating in rural areas were simultaneously at work in urban areas, where the drive to clear town centres of blacks and segregate them off into closely controlled and regimented townships beyond the established urban limits, has been propelled in large part by economic imperatives – the obstruction of petty enterprise and capital accumulation by blacks in competition with and to the detriment of whites. As in rural areas, the goal has been the establishment of white supremacy at all levels of the urban economy – although the process has often been justified in terms of health and sanitary considerations and other 'respectable fears' of the consequences of multi-racial living. And again, the real meaning of urban segregationist measures is more likely to be revealed in the oral recollections of their victims than in the self-justifications of white politicians and publicists.[8]

The transition to fully capitalist agriculture involved a range of intermediary forms, which are revealed in the oral testimony. Capitalising white farmers typically relied on members of tenant families, paid in kind, for their full-time labour force. Allowing Africans to continue producing their own subsistence in lieu of cash wages was a response not only to the resistance of blacks to total dispossession, but was also a result of the illiquidity of the farming economy, the uncertainty of yields from year to year, and the inability of farmers to compete for labour with more remunerative town employment. The emergent working class on the land in the first half of the century was a tied working class, not yet totally divorced from its own means of production, and constrained by pass laws and masters-and-servants legislation designed to reduce their manoeuvrability.[9]

Very often, as conditions of tenancy were reformulated in landlords' favour, sharecropping gave way to 'ploughing-and- sowing' contracts of one sort or another, whereby tenants had to use their own ploughing spans and implements to work the landlord's fields. So the increasing servility of blacks on the farms did not immediately imply the stripping of their productive resources – as long as they remained useful to white farmers with limited capital of their own; nor did it imply the quick transition to purely wage labour. But in the longer run, by the mid-century, white farming was becoming more capitalised and mechanised, with the aid of the state. It was the tractor that finally made tenants' trek oxen and implements dispensable. From the 1950s on, especially as the harvest has become mechanised, labour-tenant households have become increasingly redundant, and have been replaced by a smaller, more skilled, full-time, waged labour force. It was in these circumstances that the arable highveld has been cleared of many thousands of unwanted tenant families, with the active collusion of the state.[10]

But the whole process of rural dispossession was characterised by a profound contradiction. Many landowners continued to survive on the basis of black-produced surpluses, and many others (impoverished whites seeking survival on the land as well as urban entrepreneurs) actively sought out land to rent so that they could profit from the enterprise of black tenants – right up to the 1940s and even the 1950s in some parts. Herein lay the contradiction at the heart of the social transformation of the countryside: the publicly proclaimed racial idealism which swept whites into recurrent crescendos of populist fervour in pursuit of a white-dominated capitalist agriculture, contrasted sharply with the private interests of many of these same whites, landholders and lessees, who continued to rely on black tenant production for their tenuous survival on the land.[11]

It was by exploiting the contradictions between the ideal and the reality of racial domination that some blacks survived and even occasionally thrived, despite the tightening coils of white domination. In any number of ways the economic manoeuvrability of blacks, though severely limited and always on the edge of legality, was never as circumscribed as white supremacists desired. There were always gaps between the law and its implementation, between the communal perceptions of whites and their private behaviour. It was the very illegitimacy of black enterprise that created opportunities for them. It was their relative exploitability and vulnerability to dispossession that made them so profitable to whites and enabled many of them to survive more or less independently in the interstices of economic and social life.

This not only applied to farming enterprise by sharecropping tenants, filling the pockets of undercapitalised Boers and urban speculators alike, but also to the exercise of other kinds of skills, such as building (as Ndae Makume's story vividly illustrates). Their lower costs, lower expectations and the inescapably servile nature of their relationships with whites, gave them competitive advantages; and this further stoked the fires of resentment against them and against those whites under whose patronage they survived. Little wonder that so much of the black experience leaves such little imprint on the historical record; for so much of it was perforce hidden from public view. The political economy of white supremacy was always more pervious in the execution than in the conception. But the opportunities for independent enterprise were increasingly closed to all but the few. The eventual fate of almost all, sooner or later, was dispossession and displacement.

The successive waves of dispossession which swept countless black families off the land in what was increasingly becoming in fact as well as in name 'white' South Africa, were not solely due to the development of white farming, which has always been more vulnerable and less sustained than the ideology of white supremacy has pretended. The clearing of blacks not in service off white-owned land has always had a rationality and a dynamism all of its own; and as blacks who once lived and thrived on highveld farms have been piled by the hundreds of thousands into the vast rural slums of Qwa Qwa, Onverwacht, Winterveld, and Ledig, the land they left behind has often remained underutilised or unused, and the flow of failed white farmers off the land has accelerated. White survival, accumulation and profit always depended more on black-owned resources and black enterprise than whites have ever been willing to admit.

*   *   *

A recurrent issue that is raised in the life stories of obscure individuals is that of identity. These life stories throw light on the ways in which identity has been used by blacks as a means of resistance as well as abused by the authorities as a means of social control. Culture and identity are not immutable 'givens' that are inscribed in population groups, like genes, but are forged out of each individual's and each family's own experiences. Identity has always been much more flexible and instrumental in African society than is commonly realised. 'Ethnic identity' as currently understood was probably not often of direct relevance in people's lives prior to the age of literacy and Christianity. It is often our need to categorise and identify which imposes certain names on people in history, names that might have been unfamiliar to them. Large ethnic categories like Batswana or Basotho seem artificial from the vantage point of those to whom we retrospectively apply them. Even lesser categories, Bakoena for example, were often names given by outsiders to the people of a particular region who lived in a particular way. What we call 'clans' when referring to the Sotho–Tswana were perhaps more properly lineage clusters. Language was not necessarily a defining characteristic; the languages defined today were more accurately dialect clusters in the pre-literate age, shading into each other in a continuum throughout the

Sotho–Tswana region.[12]

If the traveller in the interior of South Africa at the beginning of the nineteenth century had asked a villager who he was, he would have identified himself in the way that would have seemed to him to be most appropriate: as the member of such a village, under such a headman or chief. Almost certainly he would not have given himself a label that would to the modern mind have denoted *ethnic* identity. Moreover, political communities were not ethnically defined, as in the European nation state. 'Tribal' categorisation has always been more of a European preoccupation than an historical reality; and internecine conflict in contemporary Africa is usually far more complex and far more closely related to contemporary political and social conditions than is implied in the timeless, atavistic image of 'tribal animosity', although it often takes overtly ethnic forms.

What is abundantly clear from the oral evidence is that ethnic identity in black South Africa today is not descended unchanged from the precolonial past. In many cases it has been quite consciously forged in response to the colonial impact on African communities, as a means of communal protection of resources and as a weapon of communal resistance to dispossession. Chiefly authority undoubtedly retained some purchase in the lives of many on the farms and in the towns of the highveld; but only insofar as chiefs retained some utility. However, the forms of chiefly authority were available to be exploited when required. And the utility and hence the legitimacy of chiefs increased enormously in the years leading up to and immediately following the passing of the Natives Land Act in 1913.[13]

Segregationist thought and policies in their formative stages were beginning to have an impact on black people's lives; and blacks, confronted with a rapidly developing industrial economy, responded by redefining claims to resources by defining new forms of identity. Indeed, segregationist measures as represented by the 1913 Natives Land Act created opportunities for these kinds of reformulations. For the Act was specifically designed to define and extend reserves for blacks, and chiefs with substantial followings could legitimately expect the state to recognise their claims to land. The utility of chiefs in the eyes of blacks as legitimate claimants to land increased markedly as a result, and the forms of ethnicity-building that we have witnessed here were the natural consequence.

Ethnic or clan affiliation does not survive because it is an innate characteristic of people and families or of their culture; it survives, or more accurately is recreated or reconstituted, because it is functional to the conditions of people's present lives. In South Africa it serves a purpose in a threatening world in which the rules are made by people whose primary goal is the forging and extending of white supremacy at every level of social, economic and political life. The oral evidence exposes the flexibility of black ethnic identity, and reveals just how instrumental, even artificial, ethnic affiliation has been in black South African history. In different ways blacks have used ethnicity for their own ends, just as the state has sought to use ethnic categorisation for *its* ends.[14]

Although the reserves as defined in the 1913 Act (constituting some 7 per cent of the total land area of the Union) were not extended until after the passing of the 1936 Natives Land and Trust Act (which set up the mechanism for the purchase of extra land for incorporation into the reserve areas), the rules of the game had been established in the second decade of the century.

Independent access to land was dependent on access to chiefly patronage. Only through the institution of chieftainship could access to resources be legitimated. Although clothed in the garb of 'tradition', there was in fact little historical continuity in the new foci of legitimacy and patronage that were emerging under the auspices of the industrial state in the new segregationist era – certainly on the highveld, where disruption of communities and fluidity of settlement had been very marked over the better part of a century.

In more recent decades, as the apartheid state set about 'cleaning up' the countryside, completing the work begun in 1913 by clearing land outside the reserves of blacks not in the service of whites, blacks once again began rebuilding networks of kinship and ethnicity. As old-style segregation gave way to new-style apartheid, with its preoccupation with identifying black national entities and reconstituting 'traditional' authority structures, new opportunities for creative reconstruction of genealogies and ascriptive status have come to the fore. It has not been unknown in recent years for obscure men to come forward from the townships and farms of the highveld, claiming to be the rightful heir to some chiefdom (such as the Bataung), demanding recognition of their rights to land and chiefly status within the privileged ruling elites of Qwa Qwa or Bophutha-tswana.[15]

In the nature of things, anybody who can make such claims to inherited chiefly status is bound to attract considerable popular support, from people who for the most part know little of their own ancestry, but who are the victims of dispossession. The collected genealogies as preserved in the works of Ellenberger and Macgregor are infinitely flexible, so that almost any descendant of one or other branch of the chiefly lineages of the nineteenth century can theoretically make a claim on government.[16] But it is also true that there are severe limits to the state's patronage in this regard, and the existing chiefly families (in Qwa Qwa, the Mopelis of the Bakoena and the Motas of the Batlokoa) are very reluctant to allow rivals to emerge.

The strategies of survival that blacks have employed have been enormously varied. But, in particular, urban blacks in the twentieth century have remained remarkably committed to the land, mainly because so many early avenues of black entrepreneurship have been been closed off, and more advanced avenues were monopolised by whites from the start. The insecurities of urban life under apartheid have meant that even those who are most secure against urban dispossession and ejection have often continued to channel some of their income into rural resources. The cattle herds of the Transkei, it has been found, are more commonly the property of urban dwellers with so-called 'Section 10' rights, rather than of migrants whose home base is in the reserves. The relationship between higher income-earning capacity in the urban economy and control over rural resources persists to this day.

The processes of dispossession and impoverishment have always had their ambiguities. There were always those who benefited. The apartheid system was never designed to reduce blacks to a uniform servility; it was always predicated on the rise of new classes, but along specific approved avenues that did not endanger white domination. There were always segregated, pseudo-traditionalist avenues for accumulation and the exercise of political patronage by blacks, particularly in the reserves. New elites have emerged and consolidated their position, economically and politically, with the blessing of the state. In the labour reserves and the urban townships, there are the wealthy, the privileged and the powerful – such as the tractor owners described by Petrus Pooe (who work the land of migrant families and take 90 per cent of the crop), and the urban businessmen and landlords who sit on the black township councils. The drive to co-opt such men into official structures has always been central to the state's system of racial control, and is an essential element in the current reform strategy.

* * *

What the oral record makes clear is the futility of schematic, unilinear, homogeneous images of social change.[17] Transformations are seldom as complete as they seem superficially, and social revolutions often appear in larger perspective to be strangely inconclusive. The same morbid symptoms of the old order reassert themselves long after they are supposed to have been buried in the dust of a previous epoch. Historical change tends to be cyclical, repetitious and cumulative. The 'view from below' alerts us to unexpected dimensions of social change, and reveals some of the contradictions and complexities and local variations of the processes involved.

How then do we characterise the social and economic forces that have spawned the white-supremacist rural order? When we investigate the gradually widening assertion of racial domination as it has been experienced in the lives of real individuals (rather than fixing our gaze exclusively on the political and public domain), we begin to see that this powerful social force grew out of the totality of white people's cultural perceptions – who they were and who they wanted to be – not only in purely material terms, but in terms of race, language, history, and community. These factors take on social meaning only when they form the basis of class action. Thus social class is determined by a far larger range of variables than the reductionists would have us believe. The subjective perception of class membership in white South Africa has always been shot through with racial imperatives whose origins might be lost in the distant past. And it is out of these subjective perceptions of 'class belonging' that large social forces are born, such as those which have been apparent throughout the stories told in this book, and which have had such a devastating impact on the lives of black people living on the land.

'Economic' and 'political' factors in the making of the racial order are thus not separable. There has been no 'political' cause (such as Afrikaner nationalism) that has not been at base also an economic one. Any black person who has experienced the forces of dispossession could confirm that. The rise of white populism and Afrikaner nationalism (the former shading into the latter as the twentieth century progressed) was experienced by blacks first and foremost in terms of the assertion of white control and domination over productive enterprise. Whites on the land in the early decades of the century were ideally and subjectively a 'class in the making', one that very crucially defined itself in racial terms.

The social forces at work in the stories told here and many others like them, cannot be reduced to the narrow functionalism that so often characterises explanations of South Africa's racial order. Arguments about the origins of the apartheid order have in recent times usually revolved around the question of whether racial discrimination has been functional to the interests of different economic sectors at different periods in narrow cost-benefit terms. How did segregationist/apartheid policies affect the viability and profitability of mining industry? This is the level at which much of the debate has proceeded.[18] Vulgar Marxism has locked horns with vulgar liberalism. But what has often been missing is a consideration of the larger environment in which capitalism has developed and thrived in South Africa. Government policies do not directly and unproblematically reflect the narrow, rationally conceived interests of capital or of a ruling class, or of a faction thereof. Often the state takes action to ensure compliance and to shore up the legitimacy of the system, and thereby flies in the face of powerful economic interests. Nevertheless, government policies provide the context for the total reproduction of the social and economic order as a whole. The government in a modern state is an autonomous actor with its own agenda, which serves no single master, but secures the conditions for the continued functioning of the entire social system.

From this perspective, segregationist/apartheid policies have in the past served dominant economic interests well. Capitalism has prospered in an artificially created first-world environment, buoyed up by constitutional and political stability and the absence of any unmanageable demands on the state's resources. This is what apartheid has achieved – the displacement of South Africa's massive black lumpenproletariat (created by the very forces of white capital accumulation) into rural slums in the reserves where they pose no real threat to public order or investor confidence, and the exclusion of the unenfranchised majority of South Africans from any direct call on public revenues. Of course these achievements have never been more than partial and temporary, and in the mid-1980s the limitations of such a strategy have been starkly revealed.[19] But while segregation/apartheid in its larger aspects as a social order has never been directly reducible to the requirements of capital in a narrow functional sense, it has until very recently provided an entirely sympathetic environment for the accumulation of capital and the generation of profit.

The racial order that emerged in South Africa, in urban as well as in rural areas, was an amalgam of all sorts of interests and imperatives, ranging from the cost constraints of gold mining companies, to the assertion of white control over productive processes on the maize farms of the highveld, to the drive to prevent a white lumpenproletariat from developing out of the landless and impoverished Afrikaners. Right up to the present all these interests and imperatives have maintained a rough and ready compatibility, at the expense of the great bulk of black South Africans. White politics has revolved around the issue of who should benefit from state patronage and resources (whether 'national' capital should be fostered in contradistinction to 'imperial' capital, whether Afrikaners should remain in a subordinate economic position in relation to the English, whether 'poor whites' had a special claim on the state or not); but until very recently there has never been much disagreement that blacks were to be mainly excluded from the patronage of the state and from the benefits of membership of civil society.

There are no truly impersonal forces in the lives revealed in this book. Individuals may not very clearly understand the processes of change to which they are party; but rarely are social transformations achieved without quite deliberate, conscious mobilisations of social energy by dominant groups around powerful symbols or imageries. No symbol is more potent than that of racial survival and racial threat. But in the process of struggle, the dominated are never entirely defenceless. In an infinity of ways, they are able to shape the reality of their lives, individually and collectively. It is out of struggle that new social forces are born. Indeed, the state has never entirely succeeded in its grand designs because the victims of its social-engineering policies have never willingly played the role assigned to them. It is for this reason above all others that the apartheid state is today in a state of permanent crisis.

1. For general background and more detail on the issues raised in this chapter, see T. Keegan, *Rural Transformations in Industrialising South Africa* (London, New York and Johannesburg, 1986); T. Keegan, 'The Dynamics of Rural Accumulation in South Africa: Historical and Comparative Perspectives', *Comparative Studies in Society and History*, 28, 4 (1986); T. Keegan, 'Agriculture: From Peasant Economy to Farm Economy' in Z. Konczacki, J. Parpart and T. Shaw (eds), *An Economic History of Southern Africa* (London, forthcoming), volume 2.

2. For a vivid case study of one very prominent product of the social milieu see B. Willan, *Sol Plaatje: A Biography* (London, 1984); generally, see P. Delius and S. Trapido, *'Inboekselings and Oorlams: The Creation and Transformation of a Servile Class'* in B. Bozzoli (ed.), *Town and Countryside in the Transvaal* (*Johannesburg*, 1983).

3. For a study of the radical impact of earliest industrialisation on indigenous society see K. Shillington, *The Colonisation of the Southern Tswana, 1870-1900* (Johannesburg, 1985).

4. See T. Keegan, 'The Sharecropping Economy on the South African Highveld in the Early Twentieth Century', *Journal of Peasant Studies*, 10, 2/3 (1983).

5. See S. Trapido, 'A History of Tenant Production on the Vereeniging Estates, 1890-1920' in W. Beinart, P. Delius and S. Trapido (eds), *Putting a Plough to the Ground: Accumulation and*

Dispossession in Rural South Africa (Johannesburg, 1986); T. Matsetela, 'The Life Story of Nkgono Mma-Pooe: Aspects of Sharecropping and Proletarianisation in the Northern Orange Free State, 1890-1930' in S. Marks and R. Rathbone (eds), *Industrialisation and Social Change in South Africa* (London, 1982).

6. The classic polemic on these developments is Sol Plaatje's *Native Life in South Africa* (London, 1916; reprinted Johannesburg, 1982).

7. See T. Keegan, 'Crisis and Catharsis in the Development of Capitalism in South African Agriculture', *African Affairs*, 84, 336 (1985).

8. The assertion of racial domination in the urban context is best explored by C. van Onselen, *Studies in the Social and Economic History of the Witwatersrand, 1886–1914*, 2 volumes (London and Johannesburg, 1982). A nice parallel to this process is provided by the measures designed to inhibit black transport-riding enterprise in rural areas, which were commonly justified by reference to the supposedly unhygienic condition of black-owned trek oxen and their imagined threat to the health of white-owned animals – particularly during times of epizootic such as the rinderpest of the 1890s.

9. See M. Lacey, *Working for Boroko: The Origins of a Coercive Labour System in South Africa* (Johannesburg, 1981), ch. 4.

10. See M. de Klerk, 'Seasons That Will Never Return: The Impact of Farm Mechanisation on Employment, Incomes and Population Distribution in the Western Transvaal', *Journal of Southern African Studies*, 11, 1 (1984). On forced removals of population into resettlement camps in the reserves, see the 5-volume report of the Surplus People Project, *Forced Removals in South Africa* (Cape Town, 1983).

11. See M. Nkadimeng and G. Relly, 'Kas Maine: The Story of a Black South African Agriculturist' in B. Bozzoli (ed.), *Town and Countryside in the Transvaal* (Johannesburg, 1983).

12. See T. Maggs, *Iron-Age Communities of the Southern Highveld* (Pietermaritzburg, 1976); W. Lye and C. Murray, *Transformations on the Highveld: The Tswana and Southern Sotho* (Cape Town, 1980); M. Legassick, 'The Sotho–Tswana Peoples before 1800' and W. Lye, 'The Distribution of the Sotho Peoples after the Difaqane' both in L. Thompson (ed.), *African Societies in Southern Africa* (London, 1969).

13. See T. Keegan, 'White Settlement and Black Subjugation on the South African High Veld: The Tlokoa Heartland in the

Northeastern Orange Free State, 1850-1914' in W. Beinart, P. Delius and S. Trapido (eds), *Putting a Plough to the Ground: Accumulation and Dispossession in Rural South Africa* (Johannesburg, 1986).

14. See S. Marks, *The Ambiguities of Dependence in South Africa* (Baltimore and Johannesburg, 1986).

15. The author has personal knowledge of such cases.

16. D. Ellenberger and J. C. Macgregor, *History of the Basuto* (London, 1912).

17. As represented for example in the work of M. L. Morris, 'The Development of Capitalism in South African Agriculture', *Economy and Society*, 6, 3 (1976).

18. For example, see Merle Lipton, *Capitalism and Apartheid: South Africa, 1910–1986* (Aldershot, Hants, 1986).

19. Faced with a crisis potentially much worse than the risks entailed in full democratisation, sections of the white business elite are now addressing for the first time the core element of the whole apartheid system, the issue of political power, and even seeking to open channels of communication with the African National Congress. But there is a strong possibility that once the 'siege economy' is a *fait accompli*, business will be sucked into new relations of dependence on the white government.

Oral Testimony
in the
Recovery of People's History

'What historians need are not more documents but stronger boots.'
– R. H. Tawney

This book has explored some of the rural experiences of black South Africans living on the highveld during the course of this century. Each life story told here is of course unique. But each individual's life embodies something of the common experience of a larger social group; each individual life reveals aspects of the experience of a class, of a racial or ethnic group, of a community, of a geographical region, of a particular kind of economic enterprise. Individual memory is usually an indispensable source of evidence at the historian's disposal when investigating such fields of history, given the silences of the written sources. Some people's skills of observation and recall and eye for colour and detail in their own memories of past events are greater than others'. Some people yield more information, or more usable information than others. Some people understand the larger social forces in their lives more incisively than others, and can therefore interpret and contextualise their life experiences more coherently than others. Some people's lives are more representative than others'. Often the unique or unusual or unexpected story reveals more than the unexceptional. But in the final analysis the historian is looking for patterns, not just reminiscences for their own sake.

However, we should not lose sight of the human individuals whose communal history we are trying to document. The richness and variety of the past should not be reduced to abstraction, for then it loses its human dimensions and relevance in terms of people's subjective experiences. So the purpose of this collection of life stories has been to begin to draw a portrait of what happened to rural blacks on the highveld, by examining the lives of a few isolated individuals who have interesting and revealing stories to tell, and whose recollections expose in a graphic, vivid and accessible manner larger social experiences and forces.

The stories told here are all told by men. This is of course not to imply that the experiences of women are any less important. The perspectives of women are likely to reveal different dimensions of the rural experience to that of their menfolk. The feminine viewpoint of, for example, household conflict, the experience of patriarchy, women's experiences of labour and social control, of migrancy and the processes of urbanisation, their different cultural priorities and expectations, are likely to contrast with the evidence of men. The Wits Oral Documentation Project is engaged in exploring women's life histories as a special project, involving a series of interviews with women living in the resettlement area of Phokeng in the western Transvaal, which will serve as a corrective to the patriarchal biases evident here.[1] But the difficulties of investigating women's experiences and perspectives should not be underestimated. Patriarchy itself (the domination and control of men over women) is a major obstacle; women are not supposed to view the world through independent lenses. Publicly they share the perspectives of their menfolk. Their private worlds are hidden from the outsider's view. In practice, the interviewer is likely to find that women will allow their menfolk to talk for them. Ideally, since family structure, interaction and conflict are crucial themes in the study of social history, the views of men and women, elders and juniors, in all their permutations need to be investigated.

Some might think that the subjects should be left to speak for themselves, in their own words, with editorial intervention only. In fact that is almost always impossible. Reminiscences simply do not come out as connected narratives.[2] Questions have to be constantly asked; information has to be extracted. Seldom can the informant's own words be quoted verbatim without being explained and 'translated'. Creative reconstruction by an interlocutor is necessary before the broken conversational process can be made intelligible as a narrative. What is more, the significance and meaning of much of what an informant tells us cannot really be understood unless placed in the context which only the practising historian can provide.

The ultimate reason for collecting oral histories is to understand the past more fully. It stands to reason that the greater the variety of oral evidence that one has at one's disposal, the richer, fuller and more convincing the larger social picture that emerges. But it is also true that rarely can oral testimony stand by itself as a source of evidence on the past, and it has to serve as a supplement to other, more formal, written sources of evidence (printed and documentary), which provide the larger context of public events, of political and constitutional, economic and institutional developments, in relation to which ordinary people lead their lives. Oral testimony is only a supplementary resource in the writing of history, but it is nevertheless indispensable for a full appreciation of the more recent human past. In practice, different sources of evidence, written and oral, reinforce one another, give each other meaning, explain hidden significances in each other. In the actual mechanical process of reconstructing the past, the creative imagination of the historian plays the central role in orchestrating and interpreting the diverse, contradictory, fragmentary, momentary pieces of evidence which survive.

The historian not only has to provide sufficient evidence to back his arguments (although in practice it is impossible to document every transient scrap of evidence on which he bases his conclusions), but he also has to satisfy himself as to its accuracy. It is in the footnotes that history is differentiated from art and artifice. Oral testimony, like other sources of evidence, provides problems of verification. Human memory is given to error, misconception, elision, distortion, elaboration and downright fabrication. In this (contrary to the prejudices of scholarly purists) it suffers from the same problems as much that survives in written form from the past. But the skilful historian can usually navigate these rapids with a liberal resort to the rhetorical arts of scepticism and speculation. He can generally read between the lines of the circumstantial and episodic evidence to get at the social realities beneath. Furthermore, oral evidence can in a variety of ways be tested against facts known to the researcher, or against information available, for example, in old newspapers or in archives. Public events often impinge upon people's private lives, and the accuracy of dates and places and names can often be confirmed from other sources. The trained researcher can often sense inaccuracies, hearsay or speculation in the reminiscences of his informants.

The author of this book has tried to give meaning and context to the life stories told here by using evidence and conclusions drawn from detailed research in archives and libraries. But the book does not claim to be primarily a work of scholarship. The task of synthesising different sources of evidence in larger-scale works of historical analysis is being attempted elsewhere – complete with comprehensive footnote references to satisfy the criteria of scholarship.[3] That is not the goal of this book. It is intended to serve as a more modest, accessible supplement to my previous more academically specialised book, with a view, I hope, to communicating essential processes in the making of present-day South Africa to a wider audience. As that earlier work contained detailed source references in support of the more general background analysis offered in this book as well, footnotes have been avoided here.[4]

Of course, there is a variety of ways in which historians can learn about the lives of obscure people. Social historians use all sorts of documentary sources to learn about the patterns of everyday life away from the spotlight. Censuses, police and court records and tax registers are amongst the many kinds of record which often survive and which can contain invaluable information (a consideration which has not deflected the South African government from destroying local court records indiscriminately and systematically in what amounts to a policy of intellectual vandalism). Much human history is irrecoverable; the further back one goes the more finite are the resources available for reconstructing the past. Oral testimony is more transient than almost any other window onto the past, as it is a wasting resource, and survives only as long as the person who is its custodian. But the fact remains that the recent past has left its traces in an almost limitless variety of repositories, mainly quite untapped – most obviously in the memories of a multitude of largely obscure people.

Without oral research the study of contemporary history often lacks the common touch and tends to remain a narrative of the doings of public men. The traditional sources of historical evidence – overwhelmingly relating to public affairs – dictate the traditional, rather narrow, fields of historical research (political, diplomatic, military, constitutional, institutional) with a strong bias toward the history of events rather than social analysis. Of course, no field of historical enquiry is inherently more important than any other in an intellectual sense, and the traditional concerns of academic scholars require no apologia; but escaping the narrow confines of academia is a duty not to be denied, if academic history is to engage with the larger society and not to be an elitist exercise pursued in a vacuum. A more engaged and less restricted historiography requires not only new questions and new theoretical expertise, but also new methods of research. If our investigations are to extend beyond the isolated patches of illumination under the street lamps into the large surrounding areas of darkness, we have to develop new sources of illumination. This is the role of oral research.

This is particularly the case in the study of less documented people who retain a strong rural base, such as the black people of South Africa. Social and economic patterns are infinitely varied in rural society. Modern urban life is much more susceptible to official monitoring and regulation than rural life. Urban-based industrial technology imposes a certain uniformity on economic patterns, while rural productive activities are as varied as the physical environment. The factory or workshop is relatively accessible to the historian; the rural economy less so. Yet, in order to understand the history of black people in South Africa and the larger political economy which has shaped their lives, it is essential to investigate the full dimensions of the rural experience. And again, this is unlikely to be achieved without systematic oral research of the sort reflected in this book.

In South Africa as elsewhere, there is a natural tendency amongst writers seeking the larger view of the past to rely on the readily available official sources – government publications, commission reports, legislative enactments – on the assumption that such evidence accurately reveals large-scale patterns of economic and social life and the way they change over time. But official sources of information do not provide much leverage to the historian seeking to get under the covers as it were of rural society. The short-cut approach does not work very well. Not only does it lead to a simplistic, schematic picture, but an inaccurate one. The politicians and officials whose words and perceptions are reflected in the written record were never omniscient. Indeed they are more often than not the last informants one should turn to in search of evidence about social and economic life in the past – especially in a situation in which so much economic activity takes place beyond the purview and control of the bureaucratic state. Indeed, state interventions in rural society have always been ill-informed and often ineffective. Social-engineering interventions by the state have often amounted to a declaration of social ideals more than anything else – for example in the repeated statutes seeking to abolish black rent tenancy in its various forms. Of course, the destruction of the black farming economy was eventually achieved, but the way this came to pass was altogether more complicated than is suggested by a state-centred approach to historical research and a reliance on the official voice.[5]

Indeed, in South Africa, where the dominant racial minority has always largely controlled the creation and dissemination of public knowledge and opinion, the documentary sources of evidence on the past usually contain little echo of the historical experiences of black people. What is more, in South Africa almost any consideration of black history is bound to be subversive of almost every aspect of official ideology, and much official energy in recent decades has gone into ensuring that any historical imagery incompatible with the sanitised state mythology is eliminated. The sporadic suppression of black political organisations, of black newspapers, journals and books, and the elimination of access to mission schools and independent, English-language universities with their more liberal, universalist values, have all been part of this process. The racial crudities and stereotypes of the official school history syllabuses, which deny blacks any meaningful history at all, and the close political and ideological control exercised over the state-created ethnic universities for blacks, are also part of this process.[6]

It is not surprising that few black scholars attuned to international trends in the study of African history have emerged out of such an educational system. The sad fact is that in the last fifteen or twenty years, those who have been responsible for shaking South African scholarship out of its colonial past have almost all been whites.[7] Rectifying this situation has become an urgent task and is likely to provide an indication of the capacity and willingness of the liberal universities to adapt to and accommodate post-apartheid realities in South Africa. Oral research amongst black people should ideally be performed by fully trained black scholars engaged in their own research projects, who have the linguistic expertise and racial affinity with their informants necessary to win their confidence.

The recovery of black social and economic history in all its uncomfortable dimensions and ramifications is a task of the utmost importance, not only as an academic exercise, but as a central contribution to restoring a sense of identity to people who have been stripped of any meaningful communication with the past. This does not mean that historians should sacrifice their primary commitment to scholarship as a value in itself; but no historical work takes place in a vacuum. History is a communal resource. A half-articulated, 'common-sense' history embodying common values and a common sense of identity, underpins all social groups, and is the crucial element in binding disparate classes and ethnic groups together in modern states. Communicating an accurate history in contradiction to apartheid mythology must stand high on the agenda of anyone committed to working for a new South Africa. Historians should be in the forefront of those pioneers who are charting the way into the post-apartheid future. This does not require political affiliation or any sacrifice of scholarly values; but it does require some sensitivity to the essential role of history in society – something Afrikaner nationalist historians learned a long time ago, to good effect in the mobilisation of Afrikaners and the elaboration of the apartheid state.

But there are other reasons for studying the history of obscure black people. Investigating the lives of the least privileged is not merely a matter of providing some incidental colour against which to set the main drama of history, or of extending laterally the scope of historical enquiry, or even of acknowledging different subjective experiences of history 'from below'; it is more fundamentally a challenge to our conventional understanding of the very dynamics of historical change. The fruits of oral research are more than the meat on the bones of historical reconstruction; they tend to reshape the bones themselves. In the narratives of ordinary people's lives we begin to see some of the major forces of history at work, large social forces that are arguably the real key to understanding the past, which an exclusive focus on the lives and activities of 'great men' not only obscures, but also misrepresents. The social and economic history contained in the oral record, of which this book contains only a paltry sampling, found no trace in the history texts until very recently, nor in the historical consciousness of most people; and yet its significance in reformulating and extending our understanding of the origins of modern-day South Africa is, I believe, considerable.

1. See B. Bozzoli, 'Migrant Women and South African Social Change: Biographical Approaches to Social Analysis', *African Studies*, 44, 1 (1985) on the women's project.

2. Exceptions are of course written memoirs; but they are almost always written by the educated and prominent, whose lives are largely concerned with public affairs. For an example of an extraordinary, classic autobiography of an obscure, uneducated man, based on recorded oral recollections, *see All God's Dangers: The Life of Nate Shaw*, ed. T. Rosengarten (New York, 1974). But the extent to which the words are those of the subject or the editor, whether it is genuine oral testimony or to some extent creative reconstruction written in southern dialect, remains an open question.

3. For example, T. Keegan, *Rural Transformations in Industrialising South Africa* (London, New York and Johannesburg, 1986). Charles van Onselen tackles the problem of biography in his forthcoming

study of an obscure black sharecropper from the western Transvaal, Kas Maine, which is the most ambitious project to come out of the Oral Documentation Project at Wits. Van Onselen's exhaustive oral research involving a large number of people, backed by careful work in archives and libraries, promises to result in a work much more comprehensive and scholarly than anything attempted here. If the subject has a strong, vivid, perceptive memory, there is potentially no limit to the amount of information that can be collected on any individual life. The life stories presented in this book could have been greatly expanded; but in all cases the subjects died before further interviews could take place.

4. The details of the life stories are of course drawn from the recorded interviews, as well as information gleaned when the tape recorder was turned off – information which can be surprisingly rich, imparted in informal conversation, for example over a meal, and which ideally should be committed to paper as soon as possible.

5. The points raised in this paragraph are pursued further in T. Keegan, 'Crisis and Catharsis in the Development of Capitalism in South African Agriculture', *African Affairs*, 84, 336 (1985).

6. See L. M. Thompson's *The Political Mythology of Apartheid* (New Haven, Connecticut, 1985), on the changing basis of apartheid mythology.

7. For an exception, see the work of T. Matsetela, also based on the fruits of the Wits Oral Documentation Project: e.g., 'The Life Story of Nkgono Mma-Pooe: Aspects of Sharecropping and Proletarianisation in the Northern Orange Free State, 1890-1930' in S. Marks and R. Rathbone (eds), *Industrialisation and Social Change in South Africa: African Class Formation, Culture and Consciousness, 1870-1930* (London, 1982).

Glossary

achterryer	black groom
baas	master
blesbok	antelope
bohali	bridewealth
bywoner	poor white tenant
Difaqane	period of upheaval among the black people of the highveld in the 1820s and 1830s
donga	eroded watercourse or gully
die drie dag	'three days' sickness' or Spanish influenza
field cornet	a local official similar to a justice of the peace
kgoro	ward
morena	master; Sotho title of respect accorded to chiefs
oorlams	the class of acculturated black dependants, Afrikaans-speaking and Christianised, incorporated into the Boer rural economy
oubaas	old master; a respectful form of address
samp	ground maize
volke	literally 'people'; the members of a black community on a white-owned farm
wildebees	antelope